EUROVISION REVISITED

EUROVISION REVISITED

Champions – Volume I (1956-1999)

RYAN VALMONT

© Copyright 2024 RYAN VALMONT
All rights reserved.

CONTENTS

INTRODUCTION 1
BACKGROUND 3
History 4
The Big Four/Five 5
PROFILES 7
Jon Ola Sand – "Take It Away" 7
LEADING COUNTRIES (1956 - 1999) 9
Ireland 9
United Kingdom 10
Luxembourg 11
France 12
Sweden 14
Netherlands 15
CONTEST RESULTS 1956 - 1999 17
1956 17
1957 21
1958 25
1959 28
1960 31
1961 34
1962 38
1963 41
1964 44
1965 47

1966	51
1967	56
1968	62
1969	68
1970	79
1971	87
1972	90
1973	94
1974	98
1975	105
1976	109
1977	113
1978	117
1979	121
1980	125
1981	129
1982	133
1983	138
1984	143
1985	147
1986	152
1987	156
1988	159
1989	164
1990	168
1991	172
1992	176
1993	181
1994	185
1995	191
1996	195

1997	197
1998	201
1999	206

INTRODUCTION

In the dazzling tapestry of Europe's cultural landscape, there exists a unique stage where nations come together not to wage battles but to engage in harmonious melodies, captivating performances, and an electrifying celebration of diversity. Welcome to the enthralling world of the Eurovision Song Contest, where music is the universal language, and each note is a brushstroke on the canvas of continental unity.

Behind the scenes of this grand spectacle stand visionary minds who have guided its evolution through the years. Imagine the orchestral conductor shaping the symphony of nations with a mere flick of the baton. Picture the masterful choreographer weaving together an intricate dance of emotions and stories. In the realm of Eurovision, two such figures have left an indelible mark: Jon Ola Sand and Martin Österdahl. These maestros of creativity have not only steered the contest into new eras but have also held its heart steadfast to its original ethos - a celebration of music's power to transcend borders.

And what better way to navigate the vibrant history of the Eurovision Song Contest than to dive into its contest results spanning from 1956 to 1999 **(check out volume 2 for 2000 and beyond)**

Each year, artists from across the continent have woven their melodies into the tapestry of time. From heart-stopping ballads that resonate with the soul to foot-stomping anthems that ignite the spirit, the spectrum of song successes is as wide and varied as Europe itself. The leaderboard stands as a testament to the collective artistry of these nations, where victory isn't just about taking home a trophy but about sharing a piece of one's soul with the world.

Amidst the euphoria and anticipation, one element remains constant - the scoreboard that showcases the crème de la crème of Eurovision's history. The Top 5 Entries, each a masterpiece in its own right, evoke nostalgia, triumph, and perhaps even a touch of Eurovision magic. Like timeless echoes, these songs remind us of the moments when music united us, bridging gaps and fostering bonds.

So, dear reader, prepare to embark on a journey through the heart of Europe's most spectacular musical extravaganza. A journey that will take you beyond borders, beyond language, and beyond time. From the visionary minds who sculpt its destiny to the nations that lend their voices, and from the thrilling highs of victory to the soul-stirring notes of the scoreboard, the Eurovision Song Contest invites you to immerse yourself in a symphony of culture, camaraderie, and creativity. The stage is set, the lights are dimmed, and the music is about to begin.

BACKGROUND

The Eurovision Song Contest, also known as ESC, is an annual music competition organised by the European Broadcasting Union (EBU). It brings together countries from Europe and beyond to showcase original songs performed live on television. The winner is determined through a voting process. Inspired by Italy's Sanremo Music Festival, the Eurovision Song Contest has been held every year since 1956 (although cancelled in 2020 due to the covid pandemic) and is recognised as one of the longest-running television programs worldwide. Traditionally, the host country is the previous year's winner, providing an opportunity to promote the host nation and its city as tourist destinations. While the contest has faced criticism for its perceived political aspects, extravagant stage productions, and broadcast censorship, it remains one of the most-watched non-sport events globally, often giving a significant career boost to its participants.

The European Broadcasting Union (EBU) is an esteemed alliance of public service media (PSM) organisations. It consists of 112 member groups from 56 countries and 31 Associates from various regions worldwide, such as Asia, Africa, Australasia, and the Americas. These members collectively operate nearly 2,000 television, radio, and online channels and services, offering diverse content across multiple platforms. With a combined audience of over one billion people globally, they broadcast in 153 languages. The EBU manages both the Eurovision and Euroradio services.

The EBU's rich history is worth exploring. Its mission is to ensure a sustainable future for public service media by providing high-quality content ranging from news to sports and music. The organisation builds upon its founding principles of solidarity and cooperation to foster a centre for learning and sharing.

HISTORY

The Eurovision Song Contest was established in the post-World War II era as a means to foster cooperation between European countries through cross-border television broadcasts. This initiative led to the European Broadcasting Union (EBU) formation in 1950. The term "Eurovision" was first coined by British journalist George Campey in 1951 when referring to a BBC program relayed by Dutch television. After several internationally broadcast events through the Eurovision network in the early 1950s, an EBU committee was established in 1955 to explore new avenues for cooperation among broadcasters. This eventually led to the approval of a European song competition proposed by RAI manager Sergio Pugliese. In 1955, the EBU's general assembly agreed to organise the song contest, initially titled the European Grand Prix, with the first event held in Lugano, Switzerland, in 1956. While the contest was inspired by Italy's Sanremo Music Festival, which had been running since 1951, modifications and additions were made to adapt it to an international scale.

The inaugural contest featured seven participating countries, each represented by two songs. This was the only time multiple entries per country were allowed. The winning song was "Refrain", performed by Lys Assia, representing the host country Switzerland. Voting in the first contest took place behind closed doors, but in 1957, a scoreboard was introduced, and the voting results were publicly announced. The tradition of the previous year's winner hosting the following year's contest began in 1958. Technological advancements have significantly transformed the contest over the years, introducing colour broadcasts in 1968, satellite broadcasts in 1985, streaming in 2000, and widescreen and high-definition broadcasts in later editions.

During the 1960s, the number of participating countries ranged from 16 to 18. In the 1970s and 1980s, countries from outside Europe were included. The changes in Europe following the end of the Cold War led to the addition of new countries from Central and Eastern Europe. In 1993, a separate pre-qualifying round was introduced for seven of these new countries, and a relegation system was implemented in 1994 to manage the number of competing entries. The contest expanded further in 2004 with the inclusion of a semi-final round, followed by the addition of a second semi-final in 2008.

As of 2023, Eurovision has hosted 67 contests, making it the longest-running annual international televised music competition, according to Guinness World Records. It is also listed among the world's longest-running television programs and is widely recognised as one of the most-watched non-sporting events globally. At least 52 countries have participated in the contest, with a record-breaking 43 countries competing in a single edition. In 2015, Australia became the first non-EBU member country to participate initially as a one-time occurrence for the 60th-anniversary edition but has since secured participation in subsequent years.

THE BIG FOUR/FIVE

In 1999, the European Broadcasting Union (EBU) introduced a rule allowing certain countries, namely the United Kingdom, France, Germany, and Spain, to automatically qualify for the final of the Eurovision Song Contest without going through the semi-finals. These countries, known as the "Big Four," were granted this privilege due to their substantial financial contributions to the EBU. In 2011, Italy joined the group, expanding it to the "Big Five." In 2008, there were reports suggesting that the Big Four might lose their automatic qualification status and be required to participate in the semi-finals. However, this did not come to pass, and the rule remained unchanged.

PROFILES

JON OLA SAND – "TAKE IT AWAY"

Jon Ola Sand is a Norwegian television executive known for his prominent role in the Eurovision Song Contest. He served as the European Broadcasting Union's Executive Supervisor of the Eurovision Song Contest from 2011 to 2020.

Sand was born on the 21st of December 1961 to revue writer and actor Bjørn Sand and actress Unni Bernhoft. He grew up in Vinderen, Oslo, with a brother and a sister. His brother, Simen, is an actor and author. Sand has been in a cohabiting relationship with Swedish choreographer Mattias Carlsson since May 2010. He currently resides in Geneva, Switzerland.

In terms of his career, Sand began his journey in the entertainment industry with a minor role in the 1980 film "At dere tør!" He graduated from the music branch of his local upper secondary school in the same year. Sand's passion for music led him to play the drums in a hard rock band during his teenage years. This eventually led to his employment at NRK, the Norwegian Broadcasting Corporation, as a researcher for a music TV program.

Sand's television career took off when he joined NRK in 1981. He steadily progressed from program secretary to producer and project leader, overseeing major productions and co-productions. His contributions extended to notable shows such as the Nobel Peace Prize Concert, the Amanda Award show, and the Melodi Grand Prix.

However, Sand is most renowned for his involvement in the Eurovision Song Contest. He headed the Norwegian delegation at the Eurovision Song Contest from 1998 to 2005. In 2010, he assumed the role of Executive Producer for the Eurovision Song Contest held in Oslo, Norway. Later that year, he was appointed as the European Broadcasting Union's Executive Supervisor of the Eurovision Song Contest following the resignation of Svante Stockselius. In this role, Sand had the final say in the production of the contest, including the ability to overrule the producers and give instructions. He also took charge of organising the voting system.

Sand made his debut as Executive Supervisor at the 2011 contest in Düsseldorf and went on to serve in the same capacity for the Junior Eurovision Song Contest in 2016. He spearheaded various initiatives, including the idea of a potential Worldvision Song Contest, although it did not materialise due to limited interest and high costs. Instead, the European Broadcasting Union explored exporting the Eurovision concept by launching separate versions in Asia and the United States.

Sand announced his intention to step down as Executive Supervisor of the Eurovision Song Contest after the 2020 edition, which was ultimately cancelled due to the COVID-19 pandemic. Swedish TV producer Martin Österdahl succeeded him in this role. Following his departure, Sand returned to NRK and took on the role of project leader for the relocation of its head office.

Jon Ola Sand's contributions to the Eurovision Song Contest have left an indelible mark on the event, making him a significant figure in the world of television and music production.

LEADING COUNTRIES (1956 - 1999)

IRELAND

Ireland has a rich history in the Eurovision Song Contest, having participated 56 times since its debut in 1965. The country has achieved remarkable success, sharing a joint record of seven wins with Sweden. Ireland is the only country to have won the contest three times consecutively.

The first victory for Ireland came in 1970 when Dana won with the iconic song "All Kinds of Everything." Johnny Logan, a legendary figure in Eurovision history, brought home two victories for Ireland, first in 1980 with "What's Another Year" and then again in 1987 with "Hold Me Now." Other notable winners include Linda Martin with "Why Me" in 1992, Niamh Kavanagh with "In Your Eyes" in 1993, Paul Harrington and Charlie McGettigan with "Rock 'n' Roll Kids" in 1994, and Eimear Quinn with "The Voice" in 1996. Johnny Logan also holds the distinction of writing the winning entry in 1992.

Throughout the years, Ireland has achieved a total of 18 top-five results and has finished second on four occasions. The 1990s were particularly successful for Ireland, with three consecutive victories from 1992 to 1994. However, Ireland's performance has been less remarkable in recent years, with only one top-10 placement in the last 16 contests.

Raidió Teilifís Éireann (RTÉ) serves as Ireland's representative broadcaster at the Eurovision Song Contest. The contest is broadcast in Ireland on RTÉ One, with the semi-finals aired on RTÉ2.

Ireland has hosted the contest on seven occasions, including in the capital city of Dublin. The exception was the 1993 contest, which took place in Millstreet, a small town in County Cork. All of Ireland's entries have been performed in English, except for the 1972 entry, "Ceol an Ghrá," which was sung in Irish.

UNITED KINGDOM

The United Kingdom has a long history in the Eurovision Song Contest, having participated 65 times. The country made its debut in the second contest in 1957 and has entered every year since 1959. Along with Sweden and the Netherlands, the UK is one of only three countries to have won the contest in four different decades. As one of the "Big Five" countries, the UK is automatically prequalified for the final each year due to its financial contributions to the European Broadcasting Union (EBU). The British national broadcaster, the BBC, is responsible for broadcasting the event and has used various national selection processes to choose the UK's entry.

The United Kingdom has achieved five Eurovision victories. The first win came in 1967 with Sandie Shaw's "Puppet on a String." Lulu's "Boom Bang-a-Bang" secured a victory in 1969 as part of a four-way tie. Brotherhood of Man won in 1976 with "Save Your Kisses for Me," Bucks Fizz triumphed in 1981 with "Making Your Mind Up," and Katrina and the Waves claimed victory in 1997 with "Love Shine a Light." Additionally, the UK has finished as the runner-up on a record sixteen occasions. The country has also hosted the contest a record nine times, with various cities including London, Edinburgh, Brighton, Harrogate, and Liverpool.

LUXEMBOURG

Luxembourg has a positive track record in the Eurovision Song Contest, having participated 37 times since its debut in the inaugural contest in 1956. The country only missed the 1959 contest until its last participation in 1993 but is set to make a return in 2024. With five victories, Luxembourg is one of the most successful countries in the contest. However, Luxembourg is unique among multiple winners as it has never won with an artist native to the country.

Luxembourg's first victory came in 1961 when Jean-Claude Pascal won with the song "Nous les amoureux." The country achieved back-to-back victories in the early 1970s, with Vicky Leandros winning in 1972 and Anne-Marie David in 1973. Luxembourg's fifth and most recent victory was in 1983, with Corinne Hermes winning with "Si la vie est cadeau." Following the hosting of the contest in 1984, Luxembourg faced challenges in making an impact and only managed to reach the top ten twice in subsequent years. After being relegated from participating in 1994, the country did not participate in the contest until its planned return in 2024.

Luxembourg hosted the Eurovision Song Contest four times, with all events taking place in Luxembourg City. The hosting venues included the Grand Auditorium de RTL, Villa Louvigny in 1962 and 1966, the Nouveau Théâtre in 1973, and the Théâtre Municipal in 1984. Despite its success as a host, Luxembourg's performances in the contest declined in the years following its last victory.

After Luxembourg's 1993 participation, the country faced financial and organisational issues, leading to its withdrawal from the contest. Despite occasional considerations and discussions about returning, Luxembourg did not make a comeback until the announcement in 2023 that the country would participate in the 2024 contest. RTL, the Luxembourgish broadcaster, will select the delegation for the contest through a national final.

Throughout its participation, Luxembourg predominantly selected non-native artists, with singers from France, Belgium, Greece, the Netherlands, the United Kingdom, Ireland, Germany, Spain, the United States, and Canada representing the country. Only a handful of Luxembourgish entrants participated, including Camillo Felgen, Chris Baldo, Monique Melsen, Sophie Carle, Franck Olivier, Park Café, Sarah Bray, Marion Welter, and Modern Times. Mary Christy, a Luxembourgish singer, represented Monaco in the 1976 contest, finishing in third place.

FRANCE

France has participated in the Eurovision Song Contest 65 times since its debut at the first contest in 1956. France is one of only seven countries to be present at the first contest and has been absent from only two contests in its history, missing the 1974 and 1982 shows. Along with Germany, Italy, Spain, and the United Kingdom, France is one of the "Big Five" countries that are automatically prequalified for the final due to being one of the largest financial contributors to the European Broadcasting Union (EBU). France has won the contest five times.

France first won the contest in 1958 with "Dors, mon amour", performed by André Claveau. Three more victories followed in the 1960s, with "Tom Pillibi" performed by Jacqueline Boyer in 1960, "Un premier amour" performed by Isabelle Aubret in 1962 and "Un jour, un enfant" performed by Frida Boccara, who won in 1969 in a four-way tie with the Netherlands, Spain and the United Kingdom. France's fifth victory came in 1977 when Marie

Myriam won with the song "L'Oiseau et l'Enfant". During its successful run in the 20th century, France has also finished second four times, with Paule Desjardins (1957), Catherine Ferry (1976), Joëlle Ursull (1990) and Amina (1991), who lost out to Sweden's Carola in a tie-break.

Several French broadcasters have been used to present Eurovision in the country, formerly RTF (1956–1964), ORTF (1965–1974), TF1 (1975–1981) and Antenne 2 (1983–1992). Since 1993, France Télévisions has been responsible for France's participation in the contest, with the final being broadcast on France 2 (1993–98, 2015–present) and France 3 (1999–2014).

France is one of the most successful countries in the Eurovision, winning the contest five times, coming second five times and coming third seven times. However, France has only hosted the Eurovision contest three times (1959, 1961, and 1978). France was ranked first in the number of victories (either alone or tied with other countries) without interruptions from 1960 to 1993. Moreover, Amina was close to victory with the song "C'est le dernier qui a parlé qui a raison" in 1991, when she finished in joint first place (with the same number of points as Sweden). Therefore, the 'countback' rule applied, but both countries had an equal number of twelve points (four lots). The victory went to Sweden, while France had fewer 10-point scores. Today, with the new rules, France would have won the competition because they received points from more countries than Sweden. One year before, France was also close to winning, with Joëlle Ursull performing Serge Gainsbourg's song "White and Black Blues". The song finished in equal second place with Ireland's entry.

Since their debut in 1956, France has only missed two contests, in 1974 and 1982. In 1974, after selecting a singer and song to represent them at the contest, France withdrew after the

President of France, Georges Pompidou, died in the week of the contest. If they had participated, France would have been represented by Dani with the song "La Vie à vingt-cinq ans".

In November 1981, TF1 declined to enter the Eurovision Song Contest for 1982, with the head of entertainment, Pierre Bouteiller, saying, "The absence of talent and the mediocrity of the songs were where annoyance set in. Eurovision is a monument to inanity [sometimes translated as "drivel"]." Antenne 2 took over the job due to public reaction to TF1's withdrawal, hosting a national final to select their entry.

SWEDEN

Sweden has an impressive history in the Eurovision Song Contest, having participated 62 times since its debut in 1958. The country has only missed three contests since then, in 1964, 1970, and 1976. Sweden's entries are chosen through the highly popular annual televised competition known as Melodifestivalen, which has been held since 1959.

A notable achievement for Sweden came in 1997 when it was among the first five countries to adopt televoting in the Eurovision Song Contest. The country has also hosted the contest on six occasions, with three events held in Stockholm (1975, 2000, and 2016), two in Malmö (1992 and 2013), and one in Gothenburg (1985). Sweden is set to host the contest for a seventh time in 2024, which will take place in Malmö.

Sweden has an impressive track record with 26 top-five results in the contest. The victories were achieved by notable artists such as ABBA in 1974, Herreys in 1984, Carola in 1991 and Charlotte Nilsson in 1999.

Sweden's first entry in the contest was Alice Babs in 1958, who achieved a fourth-place finish. The country's first Eurovision victory came in 1974 with ABBA's iconic song "Waterloo," which propelled the group to global fame. Throughout the 1980s, Sweden achieved three consecutive top-three results, including a victory by the Herreys in 1984 with "Diggi-Loo Diggi-Ley." Carola returned to the contest in 1991 and secured Sweden's third win with "Fångad av en stormvind." Charlotte Nilsson brought another victory to Sweden in 1999 with "Take Me to Your Heaven." The 1990s also saw two third-place finishes for Sweden.

NETHERLANDS

The Netherlands has been a participant in the Eurovision Song Contest 63 times since its debut in 1956. The country has achieved success in the competition with five victories and several top-five finishes. The Netherlands has also faced periods of non-qualification and missed contests due to various reasons.

The Netherlands' first victory came in 1957 with Corry Brokken's song "Net als toen." Teddy Scholten secured another victory for the country in 1959 with the song "Een beetje." Lenny Kuhr shared the win in 1969 with her song "De troubadour" in a four-way tie. Teach-In won in 1975 with their upbeat track "Ding-a-dong.

The Netherlands has also achieved notable results throughout its Eurovision history, including fourth-place finishes for Sandra and Andres in 1972 and Mouth and MacNeal in 1974. Maggie MacNeal secured a fifth-place finish in 1980, and Edsilia Rombley finished in fourth place in 1998.

Despite these successes, the Netherlands has faced some challenges, including occasional non-participation in the contest. The country missed the 1985 and 1991 editions due to the dates coinciding with the Dutch Remembrance of the Dead. In 1995 and 2002, the Netherlands was relegated and did not participate in the contest following poor results in previous years.

CONTEST RESULTS 1956 - 1999

1956

On the 24th of May 1956, the Eurovision Song Contest made its debut in **Lugano, Switzerland**. Organised by the European Broadcasting Union (EBU) in collaboration with the Swiss Broadcasting Corporation (SRG SSR) and Radiotelevisione svizzera (RSI), this groundbreaking event marked the beginning of an annual tradition. Dubbed the Grand Prix Eurovision de la Chanson Européenne 1956 in Italian or the Grand Prix of the Eurovision Song Competition in English, the contest took place at the Teatro Kursaal. Notably, it was the sole occasion when a solo male presenter, Lohengrin Filipello, hosted the show.

The inspiration for the Eurovision Song Contest drew heavily from the long-standing Italian Sanremo Music Festival, which had been captivating audiences since 1951. Initially proposed by the Italian broadcaster RAI, the concept of a televised song competition spanning across Europe was developed by a committee led by Marcel Bezençon, an executive from Switzerland. After receiving approval at the EBU's General Assembly in 1955, the contest's rules and structure were established. Although some of these rules were later modified in subsequent editions, the first contest featured a unique format. Each participating country presented two songs, and only solo performers were allowed to compete. Additionally, the voting process was held in secrecy, with national juries having the ability to vote for their own country's entry.

Seven countries took part in the inaugural edition of the Eurovision Song Contest. The host country, **Switzerland**, emerged victorious with the song "**Refrain**", performed by **Lys Assia**. The winner was determined by a jury consisting of two members from each participating country. Each juror awarded each song a score between 1 and 10. At the conclusion of the event, only the winning country and song were announced, while the results of the other participants remained unknown. Although the contest was broadcast on television and radio across the Eurovision network in ten countries, no video footage of the event has been discovered to date. However, audio recordings of the majority of the broadcast are available, and an independent archiver can view a reprise performance.

Lys Assia, born Rosa Mina Schärer on the 3rd of March 1924, in Rupperswil, Aargau, was a talented Swiss singer who achieved international fame. Initially starting her career as a dancer, Assia transitioned to singing in 1940 and found considerable success.

Assia secured victory and became the first-ever Eurovision champion. She later participated in the contest again in 1957 and 1958, representing Switzerland on both occasions. Beyond Eurovision, Assia found success in Germany with her hit song "O mein Papa."

Assia's remarkable career was recognised in 2005 when she performed at the "Congratulations: 50 Years of the Eurovision Song Contest" event. In 2009, she was honoured to present the Eurovision trophy alongside the previous year's winner, Dima Bilan, to the victorious artist Alexander Rybak.

In September 2011, Assia entered the Swiss national selection for the Eurovision Song Contest 2012 with her song "C'était ma vie," written by Ralph Siegel and Jean Paul Cara. Although she placed eighth in the closely contested national selection, Assia attended the event in Baku, Azerbaijan, as a guest of honour.

In 2012, Assia made another attempt to represent Switzerland at the Eurovision Song Contest 2013 in Malmö, Sweden. Her submission, "All in Your Head," featuring the hip-hop rap group New Jack, did not make it to the national selection. Rumours circulated that Assia might represent San Marino, but it was ultimately announced that Valentina Monetta would take the role. However, Assia made a guest appearance during the contest's second semi-final.

In 2015, at the age of 91, Assia made a special appearance at the Eurovision Song Contest's Greatest Hits concert, which celebrated the competition's 60th anniversary. This turned out to be her final public appearance.

Assia married Johann Heinrich Kunz on the 11th of January 1957 in Zürich. Tragically, Kunz passed away just nine months later after battling a severe illness. In 1963, Assia remarried, this time to Danish businessman Oscar Pedersen, who passed away in 1995. Lys Assia herself passed away on the 24th of March 2018 in Zürich, leaving behind a rich legacy as the first Eurovision champion.

Refrain is a captivating French song co-written by Émile Gardaz and Géo Voumard, beautifully performed by Lys Assia. "Refrain" falls into the classic chanson genre, expressing the singer's lament over lost loves during their youth. The original French lyrics mention "vingt ans," which translates to "twenty years" or "twenties" in English.

Some controversy arose regarding the voting procedures, which involved secret voting and the allowance for juries to vote for their own country's songs. Additionally, the Swiss jury voted on behalf of Luxembourg, whose juries were unable to participate.

According to the May 1956 issue of the Italian newspaper La Stampa, "Refrain" received 102 points, representing 72.8% of the theoretical maximum score each song could receive. The calculation was based on the assumption that each jury member ranked each song between 1 and 10 points, resulting in a possible total of 120 to 140 points per song, depending on whether juries could vote for their own country. Based on the rankings provided by "Hit Parade Italia," a chart that tracks the success of Italian and international songs, "Refrain" claimed the 50th position among the most successful songs in Italy in 1956.

Outside of the Eurovision Song Contest, Assia dedicated all the royalties she earned from "Refrain" to charitable causes, showcasing her generosity and philanthropic spirit.

1957

The 1957 Eurovision Song Contest marked the second edition of this annual competition. It was organised by the European Broadcasting Union (EBU) and hosted by Hessischer Rundfunk (HR) on behalf of ARD. The event took place on Sunday 3rd of March 1957, at the Großer Sendesaal des hessischen Rundfunks in **Frankfurt, West Germany** (Germany was selected to host the contest after **Switzerland declined** the opportunity to host for a second time). Hosting duties were carried out by German actress Anaid Iplicjian.

A total of **ten countries** participated in the contest. Austria, Denmark, and the United Kingdom joined the original seven countries from the previous year's contest to make their debut. Several changes were made to the rules compared to the previous edition. Each country was now represented by a single song, which could be performed by up to two artists on stage. The voting system underwent a revamp as well. Each country's jury consisted of ten individuals, with each juror having one vote for their favourite song. The voting process was conducted publicly, and a scoreboard was introduced to allow viewers and listeners at home to follow along. Notably, jurors were no longer allowed to vote for their own country's entry.

The Netherlands emerged as the winner of the contest with the song "**Net als toen**", performed by **Corry Brokken**. This marked Brokken's second appearance in the competition, as she had previously represented the Netherlands in 1956.

Corry Brokken, born Cornelia Maria Brokken on the 3rd of December 1932, was a Dutch singer, television presenter, and jurist. Throughout her career, she achieved numerous hits, performed in the popular Sleeswijk Revue alongside Snip en Snap, and hosted her own television show. Additionally, she took on the role of presenter for the Eurovision Song Contest 1976, held in The Hague, Netherlands, following Teach-In's victory the previous year. After retiring from singing in 1973, Brokken pursued law studies and became a lawyer, ultimately serving as a judge.

In 1956, Brokken emerged as the winner of the Nationaal Songfestival with the song "Voorgoed voorbij," earning the opportunity to represent the Netherlands in the inaugural Eurovision Song Contest. She shared this honour with runner-up Jetty Paerl. The following year, Brokken once again won the Nationaal Songfestival, securing her place in the Eurovision Song Contest 1957. In 1958, Brokken won the Nationaal Songfestival for the third time with the song "Heel de wereld." However, during the international final in Hilversum, the Netherlands, her entry finished in last place with only one point. Notably, John Kennedy O'Connor highlights in his book, The Eurovision Song Contest – The Official History, that Brokken is the only singer to have both won and placed last in the contest.

Following her Eurovision success, Brokken became one of the most popular female singers in the Netherlands during the 1950s and 1960s. In 1997, she announced the results of the Dutch vote for that year's contest; by that time, she had retired from singing. Having ended her musical career in 1973 to pursue law studies, Brokken became a lawyer and later served as a judge in 's-Hertogenbosch. In the 1990s, she made a comeback to the entertainment industry, performing on stage and releasing a new album. She also contributed a column to the weekly women's magazine Margriet.

Corry Brokken passed away on the 31st of May 2016 at the age of 83, leaving behind a lasting legacy in the world of music and law.

Net als toen is a poignant love song written in Dutch by Willy van Hemert and composed by Guus Jansen. Described as a nostalgic chanson, "Net als toen" features heartfelt lyrics and a melody led by the violin. The song tells the story of a wife reminiscing about the early days of her relationship with her husband, longing for the return of their lost romance. The chorus expresses her desire for their love to be rekindled, while the verses reflect on the changes that have occurred within their marriage.

"Net als toen" garnered significant support both in the Netherlands and at the Eurovision Song Contest. It received over a third of the total vote percentage in the Dutch national final before winning the international competition. The song achieved high scores from the international juries, surpassing other entries by a significant margin.

Following its Eurovision success, Brokken recorded versions of the song in multiple languages, and covers were performed by other Eurovision participants. The original Dutch single, released by Ronnex Records, achieved chart success in the Netherlands and Belgium. Over the years, "Net als toen" has been featured on numerous music compilations and commercially successful albums.

The studio version of the song is slightly shorter than its Eurovision performance, with a duration of approximately 3 minutes and 23 seconds to 3 minutes and 27 seconds. Brokken also recorded the song in French as "Tout comme avant" and in German as "Damals war alles so schön." Other artists, including Margot Eskens, Birthe Wilke, and Gunnar Thim, covered the song in German, Danish, and Swedish, respectively.

Leaderboard		
Year	Country	Victories
1957	Netherlands	1
1956	Switzerland	1

Top Scores - 1957				
Country	Artist	Song	Points	Position
Netherlands	Corry Brokken	"Net als toen"	31	1
France	Paule Desjardins	"La Belle amour"	17	2
Denmark	Birthe Wilke & Gustav Winckler	"Skibet skal sejle i nat"	10	3
Luxembourg	Danièle Dupré	"Tant de peine"	8	4
Germany	Margot Hielscher	"Telefon, Telefon"	8	4

1958

The Eurovision Song Contest returned for the third time in 1958, organised by the European Broadcasting Union (EBU) and hosted by the Nederlandse Televisie Stichting (NTS), the Dutch host broadcaster. The contest took place on Wednesday, 12 March 1958, at the AVRO Studios in **Hilversum, the Netherlands**. The Dutch television presenter Hannie Lips served as the host. This edition of the contest marked the beginning of a tradition where the host country is the winner from the previous year, with a few exceptions.

Ten countries participated, the same number as the previous year. Sweden made its debut in the contest, while the United Kingdom decided not to participate. The winning country was **France**, represented by **André Claveau**, who performed the song "**Dors mon amour**." This victory marked the first of five eventual wins for France. However, another entry had a significant impact after the contest. The Italian entry, "Nel blu, dipinto di blu", performed by Domenico Modugno, achieved third place but went on to become a worldwide hit, winning two Grammy Awards in 1959 and charting successfully in several countries.

Although the Netherlands had won the previous year, they did not automatically receive the right to host the contest. According to the convention in place at the time, each broadcaster would take turns hosting the event. The British Broadcasting Corporation (BBC) was initially chosen to host the contest in the United Kingdom but relinquished the rights due to failed negotiations with artistic unions. As a result, the Dutch broadcaster NTS was granted the opportunity to host after other broadcasters declined. This established the tradition of the previous year's winner hosting the following year's contest.

Some of the selected artists had previously competed in the contest. Lys Assia from Switzerland and Corry Brokken from the Netherlands both represented their countries in 1956 and 1957, with Brokken winning in 1957. Fud Leclerc from Belgium also competed in 1956. Margot Hielscher returned to represent Germany for the second consecutive year, having participated in 1957 as well.

André Claveau (1911–2003) was a renowned French singer active from the 1940s to the 1960s. At the age of 46 years and 76 days, Claveau became the oldest winner of the Eurovision Song Contest until 1990. He was also the first and only winner before 1990 to achieve victory in their forties.

Dors mon amour (Sleep, My Love) is a romantic love song written by Hubert Giraud and composed by Pierre Delanoë. The song, often described as a tender lullaby, gained popularity and was covered by various artists, including past Eurovision participants.

The composition revolves around the singer's expression of love, urging their beloved to sleep while reflecting on the power of their affection and the night. Its classical lullaby-like quality sets it apart from the more flamboyant and extravagant entries that would later come to define Eurovision.

"Dors, mon amour" received cover versions in French by Corry Brokken, the winner of the 1957 Eurovision contest, Achille Togliani, and Germana Caroli. It was also covered in German as "Unser Glück, mon amour" by Camillo und die Bernd Hansen-Sänger, and in Swedish as "Sov min älskling" by Alice Babs, who represented Sweden in the 1958 Eurovision Song Contest.

At the 1958 Eurovision Song Contest, "Dors, mon amour" was performed as the third entry out of ten. It gathered 27 points by the end of the voting, securing the first-place position with a three-point lead over Switzerland. Notably, it was the first winning entry to feature a male lead vocalist, following the trend set by female soloists in the 1956 and 1957 editions.

Leaderboard		
Year	Country	Victories
1958	**France**	**1**
1957	Netherlands	1
1956	Switzerland	1

Top Scores - 1958				
Country	Artist	Song	Points	Position
France	André Claveau	"Dors mon amour"	27	1
Switzerland	Lys Assia	"Giorgio"	24	2
Italy	Domenico Modugno	"Nel blu, dipinto di blu"	13	3
Sweden	Alice Babs	"Lilla stjärna"	10	4
Belgium	Fud Leclerc	"Ma petite chatte"	8	5

1959

The 1959 Eurovision Song Contest was the fourth edition of the annual event, held on Wednesday, 11th of March 1959, at the Palais des Festivals et des Congrès in **Cannes, France**. The contest was organised by the European Broadcasting Union (EBU) and hosted by Jacqueline Joubert, a French television presenter.

Eleven countries participated in the contest, with Monaco making its debut and the United Kingdom returning after a one-year absence. However, Luxembourg decided not to participate after previously competing in all the previous editions.

The Netherlands emerged as the winner with the song "**Een beetje**", performed by **Teddy Scholten**. This marked the Netherlands' second victory in the contest, having previously won in 1957. It was also the first time a country had won the contest more than once. Willy van Hemert became the first individual to win the contest twice, as he had also written the first Dutch-winning song in 1957, "Net als toen." The United Kingdom secured second place, beginning a record streak of sixteen times and finishing as the contest runners-up, while France came in third.

Among the participants, two artists had previously competed in the contest. Birthe Wilke represented Denmark in 1957, finishing third with the song "Skibet skal sejle i nat" alongside Gustav Winckler. Domenico Modugno had represented Italy in 1958, also achieving third place with "Nel blu, dipinto di blu."

Teddy Scholten (born Dorothea Margaretha van Zwieteren; 11th of May 1926) was a Dutch singer and television presenter. In 1950, Scholten received an invitation from The Coca-Cola Company to perform in the United States, making her one of the first Dutch popular music artists to do so.

Scholten collaborated with her husband, Henk Scholten, on several albums, many of which included songs for children. Throughout the 1950s and 1960s, she made appearances on popular television shows in the Netherlands. In 1965 and 1966, she served as the presenter for the Nationaal Songfestival, the Dutch national final for the Eurovision Song Contest.

Teddy Scholten passed away in The Hague on the 8th of April 2010 at the age of 83.

Een beetje is a Dutch song written by Willy van Hemert and composed by Dick Schallies. The song has a more up-tempo and light-hearted feel compared to previous winners. It tells the story of a young woman being asked by her lover if she is "true" and "faithful," to which she responds, "A little bit." The lyrics justify this admission by highlighting that everyone falls in love at least once, making it difficult to be entirely faithful to just one person. The music has a pleasant lilt to it, adding to the song's charm. Scholten also recorded versions of the song in German ("Sei ehrlich"), French ("Un p'tit peu"), Italian ("Un poco"), Swedish ("Om våren"), and an English version for British television titled "The Moment."

During the 1959 Eurovision Song Contest, "Een beetje" was performed as the fifth entry out of eleven countries. By the end of the voting, it had received 21 points, securing the first-place position.

The song received a positive reception, with Dutch newspaper Eindhovens Dagblad praising its excellent performance and fresh appeal. DutchNews.nl described it as a charming performance by Scholten, with a lively rhythm and wordplay in the lyrics that added to its musicality. The song won over the audience, even those who did not understand Dutch. However, its victory was considered surprising, as many Eurovision pundits had placed their bets on the entry from the United Kingdom performed by Pearl Carr and Teddy Johnson. They were seen as the English equivalent of Scholten and her husband.

In a retrospective review, the entertainment website Screen Rant praised "Een beetje" for its innocuous lyrics, faster pace, and energy in Scholten's performance. It noted that the song was influential and hinted at the future identity and style of the Eurovision Song Contest.

Leaderboard		
Year	Country	Victories
1957, 1959	**Netherlands**	**2**
1958	France	1
1956	Switzerland	1

Top Scores - 1959				
Country	Artist	Song	Points	Position
Netherlands	Teddy Scholten	"Een beetje"	21	1
United Kingdom	Pearl Carr & Teddy Johnson	"Sing Little Birdie"	16	2
France	Jean Philippe	"Oui oui oui oui"	15	3
Switzerland	Christa Williams	"Irgendwoher"	14	4
Denmark	Birthe Wilke	"Uh, jeg ville ønske jeg var dig"	12	5

1960

The Eurovision Song Contest 1960, the fifth edition of the annual event, took place on Tuesday, 29th of March 1960, at the Royal Festival Hall in **London, United Kingdom**. Catherine Boyle, a British television presenter and actress, hosted the contest. The European Broadcasting Union (EBU) and the British Broadcasting Corporation (BBC) organised the event, and the United Kingdom was given the opportunity to host after the Netherlands declined, having hosted the contest in 1958.

Thirteen countries participated in the competition, with Luxembourg returning after a one-year absence and Norway making its debut. **France** emerged as the winner with the song "**Tom Pillibi**", performed by **Jacqueline Boyer**. This marked France's second victory in the contest, as they had also won in 1958. The United Kingdom secured the second-place position for the second consecutive year, while Monaco achieved their first top-three finish by placing third.

Fud Leclerc represented Belgium for the third time, having previously participated in 1956 and 1958. Luxembourg's entry was the first song performed in the Luxembourgish language and one of only three entries ever performed in that language.

Jacqueline Boyer (born Eliane Ducos on the 23rd of April 1941) is a French singer and actress known for her notable achievements in the music industry. She is the daughter of renowned performers Jacques Pills and Lucienne Boyer.

At the time of her triumph at the Eurovision Song Contest, Boyer was 18 years and 341 days old, making her the first teenager to win the competition. She held the distinction of being the youngest winner until 1964. Remarkably, as of 2023, 63 years after her victory, Boyer remains the longest-surviving winning singer of the Eurovision Song Contest. It's important to note that she is not the oldest winner in terms of age, as there have been winners who have lived longer after their victories.

Tom Pillibi is a French song written by Pierre Cour and composed by André Popp. The original lyrics of the song describe a moderately up-tempo narrative about the singer's lover, Tom Pillibi. She talks about his material wealth, including two castles and ships, and mentions other women who desire him. However, she confesses that he has a significant flaw - being a compulsive liar - and admits that none of her previous statements about him were true. Despite this, she sings that she still loves him.

In the English version of the song, which became more common in Eurovision history, the portrayal of Tom differs. He is depicted as a womanizer who cannot be trusted. As a result, there is some confusion regarding the interpretation of the song. Nonetheless, Jacqueline Boyer also recorded a German-language version of "Tom Pillibi" under the same title.

During the Eurovision Song Contest, "Tom Pillibi" was performed as the thirteenth entry of the night, following Italy's Renato Rascel with "Romantica." At the conclusion of the voting, it received 32 points, securing the first-place position among 13 participants.

"Tom Pillibi" holds the distinction of being the first Eurovision winner to be performed last, which has been noted as a potential bias for recency in the contest, as pointed out by entertainment website Screen Rant.

The popularity of "Tom Pillibi" led to numerous cover versions, including one by acclaimed actress and singer Julie Andrews, who recorded the song in English in April 1960. Additionally, Laila Kinnunen, a popular Finnish singer and Finland's Eurovision debutante in 1961, recorded a Finnish version on the 14th of June 1960. Inger Berggren, Sweden's Eurovision representative in 1962, also recorded a version of the song.

Leaderboard		
Year	Country	Victories
1958, 1960	**France**	**2**
1957, 1959	Netherlands	2
1956	Switzerland	1

Top Scores - 1960				
Country	Artist	Song	Points	Position
France	Jacqueline Boyer	"Tom Pillibi"	32	1
United Kingdom	Bryan Johnson	"Looking High, High, High"	25	2
Monaco	François Deguelt	"Ce soir-là"	15	3
Norway	Nora Brockstedt	"Voi-voi"	11	4
Germany	Wyn Hoop	"Bonne nuit ma chérie"	11	4

1961

The Contest of 1961 marked the 6th edition of the annual event. In 1959, the competition returned to the charming coastal city of **Cannes. France**. It was organised by the European Broadcasting Union (EBU) and hosted by Radiodiffusion-Télévision Française (RTF). The date for this year's contest was Saturday 18th of March, making it the first time the event took place on a Saturday evening, a tradition maintained since then (with the exception of 1962). The show was skilfully directed by Marcel Cravenne and charmingly hosted by Jacqueline Joubert, who also hosted the 1959 edition.

A total of **sixteen countries** participated in the contest, three more than the previous year. Finland, Spain, and Yugoslavia made their debut appearances in the competition.

The well-deserved winner of the 1961 Eurovision Song Contest was **Luxembourg**, represented by **Jean-Claude Pascal** with the song "**Nous les amoureux**." The United Kingdom secured second place, marking the third consecutive year of finishing as runners-up.

Some returning artists from previous years included Belgium's Bob Benny and Norway's Nora Brockstedt, making their second appearances in the competition. Benny had previously represented Belgium in 1959, while Brockstedt represented Norway for the second consecutive year. In 1961, Benny returned with the song "Hou toch van mij," while Brockstedt presented "Voi Voi," following her performance from the previous year.

Jean-Claude Pascal was born in Paris to a well-off family engaged in the textile manufacturing business. His mother,

Arlette Lemoine, hailed from a lineage that included the renowned English fashion designer Charles Frederick Worth. Tragically, his father, Roger Villeminot, passed away in the same year of Jean-Claude's birth. He commenced his secondary education at the Collège Annel in Compiègne in 1938 and later completed it at the Lycée Janson-de-Sailly in Paris. In 1944, at the age of 17, he joined the 2nd Armored Division of General Leclerc, becoming the first French soldier to enter Strasbourg in November 1944 while the German Army was still evacuating the city. For this courageous act, he was awarded the Croix de Guerre in 1945.

Having survived World War II in Strasbourg, Jean-Claude pursued studies at the Sorbonne before venturing into fashion designing for Christian Dior. It was during his work on costumes for a theatre production of Don Juan that he discovered his passion for acting. He made his debut as an actor in the film "Le jugement de Dieu" (1949, released in 1952) and went on to appear in "Le rideau cramoisi" (1951) alongside Anouk Aimée, followed by several other films such as "Die schöne Lügnerin" ('Beautiful Liar,' also known as "La Belle et l'empereur") in 1959 with Romy Schneider and "Angelique and the Sultan" ('Angélique et le sultan') in 1968 with Michèle Mercier.

In a later Eurovision appearance in 1981, he represented Luxembourg once again, finishing 11th out of 20 contestants with the song "C'est peut-être pas l'Amérique" ('It may not be America'), for which he composed both the words and music in collaboration with Sophie Makhno and Jean-Claude Petit.

Jean-Claude Pascal passed away in Clichy, Hauts-de-Seine, at the age of 64 due to stomach cancer, leaving behind a legacy of talent and artistry.

Nous les amoureux, also known as "We, the Lovers" or "Us Lovers," took the fourteenth spot in the running order at the 1961 competition (following Denmark's Dario Campeotto with "Angelique" and preceding the United Kingdom's The Allisons with "Are You Sure?"), the song received 31 points by the end of the voting, securing the first position among 16 contenders. This victory allowed Luxembourg to achieve the rare distinction of moving from last place to first in consecutive years.

The song's poignant lyrics portray a love story thwarted by external forces ("they would like to separate us, they would like to hinder us from being happy"). However, it also expresses hope that their love will eventually overcome all obstacles ("but the time will come. [...], and I will be able to love you without anybody in town talking about it. [...] [God] gave us the right to happiness and joy."). Jean-Claude Pascal later revealed that the song's inspiration stemmed from a homosexual relationship and the challenges it faced. Given that addressing such a topic would have been controversial during the early 1960s, the lyrics were kept ambiguous, deliberately avoiding specific references to the lovers' gender. Consequently, the song's true message remained hidden and was not widely understood by the general public at that time.

Due to the contest running over time, the reprise of "Nous les amoureux" was not broadcast in the UK. The UK's coverage ended shortly after the voting concluded and the winning song was announced.

"Nous les amoureux" was composed by Jacques Datin and had lyrics by Maurice Vidalin. Additionally, the song was featured in Season 2, Episode 6 of the television series "A Very Secret Service."

Leaderboard

Year	Country	Victories
1958, 1960	France	2
1957, 1959	Netherlands	2
1961	**Luxembourg**	**1**
1956	Switzerland	1

Top Scores - 1961

Country	Artist	Song	Points	Position
Luxembourg	Jean-Claude Pascal	"Nous les amoureux"	31	1
United Kingdom	The Allisons	"Are You Sure?"	24	2
Switzerland	Franca di Rienzo	"Nous aurons demain"	16	3
France	Jean-Paul Mauric	"Printemps (avril carillonne)"	13	4
Denmark	Dario Campeotto	"Angelique"	12	5
Italy	Betty Curtis	"Al di là"	12	5

1962

The 7th edition of the annual Eurovision Song Contest took place in **Luxembourg City, Luxembourg**, in 1962. The European Broadcasting Union (EBU) and the host broadcaster, Compagnie Luxembourgeoise de Télédiffusion (CLT), organised the contest, which was held at the Villa Louvigny on Sunday 18th of March 1962. The Luxembourgish speaker, Mireille Delannoy, hosted the show.

Remarkably, this was the last time the final of the Eurovision Song Contest was not held on a Saturday. From 1963 onwards, the final has consistently taken place on a Saturday evening.

The contest featured **sixteen countries**, the same number as the previous year. **France** emerged as the winner with the song "**Un premier amour**," performed by **Isabelle Aubret**. This marked France's third victory in the contest within a span of just five years, having also won in 1958 and 1960. Additionally, it was the third consecutive winning song performed in French.

A notable occurrence during the 1962 Eurovision Song Contest was that Austria, Belgium, Netherlands, and Spain all scored zero points for the first time in the contest's history.

Isabelle Aubret, originally named Thérèse Coquerelle, is a renowned French singer, born on 27th July 1938 in Lille, France. Isabelle was the fifth of eleven children in her family. Her father worked as a foreman in a spinning mill, while her mother, of Ukrainian descent, was a homemaker. As a child, Isabelle trained in gymnastics and won the national French Gymnastics Championship in 1952. After leaving school in the same year, she worked as a winder in a factory in Saint-André, where her father was employed.

Isabelle's artistic journey began when she started singing in the theatre at her family's house for a radio program, returning to the spinning mill where she had previously worked. She also received training in drama and classical dance and participated in local singing competitions. Her talent caught the attention of the director of a Lille radio station, leading to her first stage appearance as a singer. In 1956, at the age of eighteen, she joined an orchestra in Le Havre. In 1960, Isabelle won a singing competition at the Olympia, where she was discovered by Bruno Coquatrix, the venue's director. After securing a cabaret spot in Pigalle, she released her debut single, "Nous les Amoureux", in 1961, adopting the stage name Isabelle Aubret.

Isabelle's career reached new heights when she emerged as the winner of the 1962 Eurovision Song Contest, which cemented her fame across Europe. However, in 1963, a car accident left her severely injured, hampering her opportunity to star in the film Les parapluies de Cherbourg, offered to her by director Jacques Demy and musician Michel Legrand.

Despite the setback, Isabelle made a triumphant return to Eurovision in 1968, once again representing France with the song "La source," composed by Daniel Faure with lyrics by Henri Dijan and Guy Bonnet.

Isabelle continued to participate in the French national heats for Eurovision in subsequent years, achieving notable successes as well as some disappointments. Throughout her career, she collaborated with French composer Michel Colombier and co-produced the song "C'est Ainsi Que Les Choses Arrivent" for Jean-Pierre Melville's 1972 film Un Flic.

Despite facing personal challenges, including a trapeze accident in 1981 that led to a two-year rehabilitation period, Isabelle Aubret's dedication and talent allowed her to celebrate a remarkable forty-year career with a series of concerts at Bobino in 2001.

Un premier amour ("A First Love") was written by Roland Valade and composed by Claude Henri Vic.

During the Eurovision competition, the song was performed ninth, following the Netherlands' De Spelbrekers with "Katinka" and preceding Norway's Inger Jacobsen with "Kom sol, kom regn". When the voting concluded, " Un premier amour " had amassed an impressive 26 points, securing its position as the top song among 16 contenders.

This beautiful ballad is characterised by its emotional and dramatic qualities, with Aubret's powerful vocals expressing the impact of first love on people's hearts.

Leaderboard		
Year	Country	Victories
1958, 1960, 1962	France	3
1957, 1959	Netherlands	2
1961	Luxembourg	1
1956	Switzerland	1

Top Scores - 1962				
Country	Artist	Song	Points	Position
France	Isabelle Aubret	"Un premier amour"	26	1
Monaco	François Deguelt	"Dis rien"	13	2
Luxembourg	Camillo Felgen	"Petit bonhomme"	11	3
Yugoslavia	Lola Novaković	"Ne pali svetla u sumrak"	10	4
United Kingdom	Ronnie Carroll	"Ring-A-Ding Girl"	10	4

1963

The Eurovision Song Contest of 1963 marked the eighth edition of this annual event and was held in **London, United Kingdom**. Organised by the European Broadcasting Union (EBU), the British Broadcasting Corporation (BBC) hosted the contest at the BBC Television Centre on Saturday, 23rd March 1963. The decision to host the contest in London came after France, the winner of the 1962 edition, declined to host it due to financial constraints despite having hosted the competition in 1959 and 1961.

Katie Boyle hosted the contest for the second time, guiding the audience through an evening filled with performances from **sixteen countries**, the same ones that had participated in the previous year.

The victorious country that year was **Denmark**, with the song "**Dansevise**," performed by **Grethe and Jørgen Ingmann**. This win marked the first-ever victory for any of the Nordic countries in the Eurovision Song Contest. However, four countries received no points: Finland, Norway, and Sweden failed to score any points for the first time, while the Netherlands experienced this for the second consecutive year, becoming the first country to go two years without receiving a single point.

Jørgen Ingmann was born on 26th April 1925 in Copenhagen, Denmark, while **Grethe Clemmensen** was born on 17th June 1938, also in Copenhagen. The couple met in 1955, married in 1956, but later divorced in 1975.

Jørgen Ingmann found significant success in the United States with his rendition of Jerry Lordan's instrumental track "Apache," which reached No.1 on the US Singles chart in 1961. Interestingly, the popularity of Jørgen Ingmann's cover was partly attributed to EMI's delay in releasing The Shadows' original 1960 version in the USA. As a result, Jørgen Ingmann's version gained momentum, surpassing The Shadows' hit in the American market. Jerry Lordan continued to write several instrumental hits for The Shadows, such as "Wonderful Land," "Atlantis," and "Maroc 5," but the band struggled to make a significant breakthrough in the US, even during the era of the "British Invasion" in the mid-1960s.

Tragically, Grethe Ingmann became the first Eurovision winner to pass away when she succumbed to cancer in August 1990 in Denmark. Jørgen Ingmann also passed away in March 2015.

Dansevise (Dance Song) is a sophisticated ballad, with the singer expressing admiration for the joy of dancing, especially with a beloved friend. The music was composed by Otto Francker, and the lyrics were written by Sejr Volmer-Sørensen. This was the first entry performed by a duo to win the contest and the first Scandinavian win.

Leaderboard		
Year	Country	Victories
1958, 1960, 1962	France	3
1957, 1959	Netherlands	2
1963	**Denmark**	**1**
1961	Luxembourg	1
1956	Switzerland	1

Top Scores - 1963				
Country	Artist	Song	Points	Position
Denmark	Grethe & Jørgen Ingmann	"Dansevise"	42	1
Switzerland	Esther Ofarim	"T'en va pas"	40	2
Italy	Emilio Pericoli	"Uno per tutte"	37	3

United Kingdom	Ronnie Carroll	"Say Wonderful Things"	28	4
France	Alain Barrière	"Elle était si jolie"	25	5
Monaco	Françoise Hardy	"L'Amour s'en va"	25	5

1964

The 9th edition of the Eurovision Song Contest in 1964 was held in **Copenhagen, Denmark**. The event was organised by the European Broadcasting Union (EBU) and hosted by Danmarks Radio (DR). The venue for the contest was the Tivolis Koncertsal (Tivoli Concert Hall), situated within the renowned amusement park and pleasure garden, Tivoli Gardens. The contest took place on 21st March 1964 and was elegantly hosted by Danish TV presenter Lotte Wæver.

Sixteen countries participated in the competition, with Portugal making its debut this year. However, Sweden decided not to enter due to a strike among members of the Swedish Union for Performing Arts and Film (Teaterförbundet). Nevertheless, Sweden's broadcaster, Sveriges Radio, ultimately broadcasted the event despite not competing.

The triumphant winner of the contest was **Italy**, with the song "**Non ho l'età**," performed by **Gigliola Cinquetti**. It was a notable year for several countries in the contest. Portugal's debut entry unfortunately resulted in them scoring zero points. Additionally, Germany, Switzerland, and Yugoslavia also scored zero points for the first time. The Netherlands made history by sending Anneke Grönloh, a singer of non-European ancestry with Indonesian heritage. Spain chose to send the Italian-Uruguayan group Los TNT, making them the first group of three or more participants.

Gigliola Cinquetti, born Giliola Cinquetti on 20th December 1947, is a renowned Italian singer, songwriter, and television presenter. Coming from a privileged background, she showed an early passion for music and art, studying piano from ages 9 to 13 and excelling in music theory exams.

Cinquetti's artistic prowess extended to various languages and cultures. Her song "Alle porte del sole," released in 1973, was re-recorded in English and Italian by Al Martino and became a top hit in the United States. She also released an English version of the song herself in 1974, titled "To the Door of the Sun."

In the Eurovision Song Contest 1974, Cinquetti returned to represent Italy with the song "Sì" ("Yes"). However, the live telecast of her performance was banned in Italy by the national broadcaster RAI due to concerns that the repeated word 'Sì' in the song could be perceived as a subliminal message influencing the upcoming Italian divorce referendum. Despite the censorship, her song reached No.8 on the UK Singles Chart in its English version, titled "Go (Before You Break My Heart)."

Beyond her music career, Cinquetti pursued education and later became a professional journalist and TV presenter. She co-hosted the Eurovision Song Contest 1991 with Toto Cutugno, celebrating her previous victory in the contest twenty-six years prior.

In 2008, she received a prestigious award honouring her remarkable career in Italy and worldwide. Additionally, Cinquetti authored an autobiography in 2014.

Recently, in the 2022 Eurovision Song Contest held in Turin, she triumphantly returned to the stage as an interval act, performing her iconic song "Non ho l'età."

Non ho l'età (I'm not old enough (to love you)") was the twelfth song performed at the 1964 contest, following Portugal's António Calvário with "Oração" and preceding Yugoslavia's Sabahudin Kurt with "Život je sklopio krug." The heartfelt ballad resonated with audiences, earning it 49 points and securing the first position among 16 competitors.

The song's success extended far beyond the Eurovision stage. It became a commercial sensation for Cinquetti in Italy, Europe, Scandinavia, and various other countries worldwide. She also recorded versions of the song in multiple languages, including English ("This is my prayer"), Spanish ("No tengo edad"), French ("Je suis à toi"), German ("Luna nel blu"), and Japanese ("Yumemiru omoi"). Many other artists have since covered the song in various languages, showcasing its universal appeal.

Leaderboard		
Year	Country	Victories
1958, 1960, 1962	France	3
1957, 1959	Netherlands	2
1964	**Italy**	**1**
1963	Denmark	1
1961	Luxembourg	1
1956	Switzerland	1

Top Scores - 1964				
Country	Artist	Song	Points	Position
Italy	Gigliola Cinquetti	"Non ho l'età"	49	1
United Kingdom	Matt Monro	"I Love the Little Things"	17	2
Monaco	Romuald	"Où sont-elles passées"	15	3
Luxembourg	Hugues Aufray	"Dès que le printemps revient"	14	4
France	Rachel	"Le Chant de Mallory"	14	4

1965

The 1965 Eurovision Song Contest marked its milestone tenth edition and took place in **Naples, Italy**. Organised by the European Broadcasting Union (EBU) and hosted by Radiotelevisione italiana (RAI), the contest was held at the Sala di Concerto della RAI on 20th March 1965, with Italian singer Renata Mauro as the host.

A record-breaking **eighteen countries** participated in the competition, making it the highest number of entrants in the contest up to that point. Sweden made a return after being absent from the previous edition, while Ireland made its debut appearance.

Luxembourg claimed victory for the second time with the song "**Poupée de cire, poupée de son**," sung by the French singer **France Gall**. The song sparked controversy but went on to become a massive hit across nearly all European countries. It marked a departure from the usual ballad-winning songs, being the first pop song ever to win the competition. However, the infamous streak continued, with four countries, namely Belgium, Finland, Germany, and Spain, receiving zero points for the fourth consecutive year, making it the second time in the contest's history that they had finished with no points.

France Gall, whose birth name was Isabelle Geneviève Marie Anne Gall, was a renowned French yé-yé singer. Born on 9th October 1947, in Paris, she hailed from a musically inclined family. Her father, Robert Gall, was a lyricist who wrote songs for prominent artists like Édith Piaf and Charles Aznavour, while her mother, Cécile Berthier, was also a singer and the daughter of

Paul Berthier, co-founder of Les Petits Chanteurs à la Croix de Bois.

At the age of 16, in the spring of 1963, France's father encouraged her to record songs and send the demos to music publisher Denis Bourgeois. This led to her being signed by Philips, with Bourgeois acting as her artistic director; she recorded several tracks with the jazz musician and composer Alain Goraguer.

Her debut single, "Ne sois pas si bête" ("Don't Be So Stupid"), released in November 1963, became a hit and sold 200,000 copies. She continued her successful run with songs like "N'écoute pas les idoles," "Laisse tomber les filles," and "Christiansen," all written by Serge Gainsbourg.

France Gall's early career featured a blend of musical styles, including jazz and pop, and she made successful appearances in Germany during the late 1960s and early 1970s.

In 1973, she collaborated with singer-songwriter Michel Berger, and they fell in love, eventually marrying in 1976. France Gall exclusively sang songs written by Berger until his death in 1992.

Throughout her career, France Gall participated in various musicals and humanitarian projects, using her talent to raise awareness for causes like famine relief in Africa. She achieved significant success with songs like "Ella, elle l'a" and "Résiste."

Tragedy struck when their daughter Pauline was diagnosed with cystic fibrosis and passed away in 1997, following the death of Michel Berger in 1992.

France Gall's musical career continued with some hiatuses, and she released her final album, "France," in 1996. In her later years, she remained relatively private, making occasional public appearances.

France Gall passed away in January 2018 at the age of 70 after battling cancer. She was laid to rest alongside her husband and daughter at Montmartre Cemetery in Paris, leaving behind a rich musical legacy.

Poupée de cire, poupée de son is a captivating song penned by Serge Gainsbourg. Gainsbourg's poetic lyrics are filled with double meanings, clever wordplay, and subtle puns, characteristic of his unique style. The title itself, "poupée de cire, poupée de son," can be translated as "wax doll, rag doll," conjuring images of a floppy doll filled with bran or chaff. However, it can also imply "wax doll, sound doll," suggesting that Gall is like a "singing doll" whose strings are pulled by Gainsbourg.

The song delves into the ironies and complexities of the baby pop genre, where young singers like Gall provide songs that explore life and love, even though they themselves may still be inexperienced. Gainsbourg's shrewdly crafted lyrics play with this idea as he weaves a tale of a singing doll whose heart resides in her songs, living life through the rose-coloured glasses of her music.

Leaderboard		
Year	Country	Victories
1958, 1960, 1962	France	3
1961, 1965	**Luxembourg**	**2**
1957, 1959	Netherlands	2
1964	Italy	1
1963	Denmark	1
1956	Switzerland	1

Top Scores - 1965

Country	Artist	Song	Points	Position
Luxembourg	France Gall	"Poupée de cire, poupée de son"	32	1
United Kingdom	Kathy Kirby	"I Belong"	26	2
France	Guy Mardel	"N'avoue jamais"	22	3
Austria	Udo Jürgens	"Sag ihr, ich lass sie grüßen"	16	4
Italy	Bobby Solo	"Se piangi, se ridi"	15	5

1966

The 1966 Eurovision Song Contest marked the 11th instalment of the annual event. It was held in **Luxembourg City, Luxembourg**, as a result of Luxembourg's victory in the 1965 competition. The European Broadcasting Union (EBU) and the host broadcaster Compagnie Luxembourgeoise de Télédiffusion (CLT) coordinated the event, which took place at Villa Louvigny on 5th March 1966. The presenter for the evening was Josiane Chen, a television personality from Luxembourg.

Eighteen countries participated in the competition, the same number as the previous year.

The victor was **Austria**, presenting the song "**Merci, Chérie**," which was both composed and performed by **Udo Jürgens**, with lyrics co-written by Jürgens and Thomas Hörbiger. Impressively, this marked Udo Jürgens' third consecutive participation in the contest, and he finally secured a win for his home country, Austria.

Austria would not claim another victory until the 2014 edition. Additionally, this triumph was noteworthy as it marked the first instance of a winning song performed in the German language. The event's outcome carried historical significance for several nations. Austria, Sweden, Norway, and Belgium achieved their best results up to that point, some of which remained unmatched for many decades. Conversely, longstanding Eurovision powerhouses such as France, the United Kingdom, and Italy experienced their worst placements up to that juncture, prompting significant disappointment among the citizens of these countries.

The stipulation that participants could only perform in their respective national languages was introduced this year. This regulation was potentially influenced by the use of English in the 1965 entry from Sweden.

Jürgen Udo Bockelmann, born on 30th September 1934, was a prominent Austrian composer and singer of popular music who enjoyed a career spanning over five decades. Across his prolific career, he composed nearly 1,000 songs and achieved sales of over 104 million records. Notably, in 2007, he acquired Swiss citizenship and subsequently legally altered his name to Udo Jürgens Bockelmann in 2010.

He is widely acknowledged for revolutionising German-language pop music beyond the conventional post-war "Schlager" style of the 1950s. He infused it with modern pop allure and elements of French chanson. His innovative compositions and arrangements resonated with audiences of all age groups. He continued to captivate audiences in Germany, Austria, and Switzerland until his death at the age of 80 in December 2014.

In 1952, under the name Udo Bolan, he established the Udo Bolan Quartet in Klagenfurt, Austria. The group regularly performed at Café Obelisk in Klagenfurt, featuring Englishman Johnny Richards on drums, Klaus Behmel on guitar, and Bruno Geiger on bass. The quartet gained popularity through appearances at diverse dance and jazz venues. They were also featured on Radio Alpenland and the British Forces Radio network, produced by Mike Fior.

In 1950, he emerged victorious in a composition contest organised by Austria's public broadcasting channel ORF with his song "Je t'aime". He penned the globally recognised 1961 hit "Reach for the Stars," famously sung by Shirley Bassey.

Jürgens made his debut representing Austria at the Eurovision Song Contest in 1964 with the song "Warum nur, warum?", securing the sixth position. His song "Sag ihr, ich lass sie grüßen" achieved fourth place in the 1965 contest. His perseverance paid off when he clinched victory at the Eurovision Song Contest 1966 in Luxembourg with "Merci, Chérie."

In the subsequent years, Jürgens crafted notable songs like "Griechischer Wein," "Aber bitte mit Sahne," "Mit 66 Jahren," and the immensely successful "Buenos Días, Argentina," which he performed alongside the German national football team during the 1978 event in Argentina.

In 1977, he invited The Supremes to appear as guests on his televised and recorded gala concert, resulting in memorable performances and collaborations. Jürgens' influence extended into the late 20th and early 21st centuries, with achievements like his disco album "Udo '80" in 1979 and his significant role in inspiring the creation of the label OBEY Clothing by Shepard Fairey.

His legacy persisted through the jukebox musical "Ich war noch niemals in New York" in 2007, which integrated Jürgens' songs into a family-oriented narrative, akin to the approach taken with ABBA songs in "Mamma Mia!" Jürgens' fame transcended borders, especially in Argentina, where he garnered a substantial fan base.

From 2015 onwards, Jürgens secured the global record for the longest duration of chart presence, spanning over 57 years from his initial entry in 1958 to 2015. A posthumous album of his works, released by his children on 16th December 2022, claimed the number one spot on the German charts on 24th December. This remarkable accomplishment signifies Jürgens' enduring impact on the German music scene for more than eight decades.

Merci, Chérie (translating to "Thank you, darling" in English) is a poignant ballad expressing the singer's gratitude to his departing lover, reminiscing about the joyful moments and fond memories they shared.

Taking the stage as the ninth performance of the evening, it followed Portugal's Madalena Iglésias with "Ele e ela" and preceded Sweden's Lill Lindfors and Svante Thuresson with "Nygammal vals." "Merci, Chérie" achieved a final points total of 31, securing the coveted first place amidst a field of 18 entries.

This victory in 1966 remained Austria's sole triumph in the Eurovision Song Contest until 2014 when Conchita Wurst achieved victory with the song "Rise Like a Phoenix." Udo Jürgens held the distinction of being the last solo male pianist to secure victory until Duncan Laurence claimed the title in 2019 with "Arcade."

Udo's rendition of "Merci, Chérie" is not confined to a single language; he recorded versions in French, Japanese (メルシー・シェリー "Merushī sherī"), English, Italian (with an adaptation by Vito Pallavicini), and Spanish (with an adaptation by Arturo Kaps-Schönfeld).

\multicolumn{3}{c}{Leaderboard}		
Year	Country	Victories
1958, 1960, 1962	France	3
1961, 1965	Luxembourg	2
1957, 1959	Netherlands	2
1966	**Austria**	1
1963	Denmark	1
1956	Switzerland	1

\multicolumn{4}{c}{**Top Scores - 1966**}
Country	**Artist**	**Song**	**Points**	**Position**
Austria	Udo Jürgens	"Merci, Chérie"	31	1
Sweden	Lill Lindfors & Svante Thuresson	"Nygammal vals"	16	2
Norway	Åse Kleveland	"Intet er nytt under solen"	15	3
Belgium	Tonia	"Un peu de poivre, un peu de sel"	14	4
Ireland	Dickie Rock	"Come Back to Stay"	14	4

1967

The 12th edition of the annual Eurovision Song Contest occurred in **Vienna, Austria**, on 8th April 1967. Organised by the European Broadcasting Union (EBU) and hosted by Österreichischer Rundfunk (ORF), the event was held at the Großer Festsaal der Wiener Hofburg. This marked the first time the contest was held in April and was presented by Austrian actress Erica Vaal.

Seventeen countries participated in this edition, one less than the record eighteen in the previous years. Denmark chose not to participate, returning only in 1978. The **United Kingdom** achieved its first victory in the contest with the song "**Puppet on a String**," performed by **Sandie Shaw**. The margin of victory was notably wide, with the UK earning more than twice the points of the second-placed song. Despite Shaw's initial dislike for the song, she later softened her attitude towards it, even releasing a new version in 2007.

Luxembourg's entry, "L'amour est bleu," performed by Vicky Leandros, secured fourth place but became a significant hit following the contest. It was later transformed into an instrumental hit titled "Love Is Blue" by French musician Paul Mauriat. Portugal's representative, Eduardo Nascimento, made history as the first black male singer to participate in the contest.

The stage setup for this year's contest was unique, featuring a central staircase and two revolving mirrored walls on either end of the stage. These walls began to revolve at the start of each song and stopped at its conclusion. A rule change required half of each nation's jury to be under 30 years old.

During the voting process, presenter Erica Vaal became confused and prematurely declared the United Kingdom's entry as the winner before Ireland had announced its votes. The programme ended with Vaal congratulating the winning song and country while bidding farewell in multiple languages. This edition also marked the last time the contest was transmitted solely in black and white, as colour transmissions began in the following year's contest.

Sandie Shaw MBE, born Sandra Ann Goodrich on 26th February 1947, is a retired English pop singer celebrated for her remarkable contributions to the music industry. An iconic figure of the 1960s, she achieved significant success with a string of hit singles. Notably, she secured three UK number-one singles: "(There's) Always Something There to Remind Me" (1964), "Long Live Love" (1965), and "Puppet on a String" (1967). In 1984, her cover of the Smiths' song "Hand in Glove" marked her return to the UK Top 40 after 15 years. Shaw retired from the music industry in 2013.

Sandra Ann Goodrich was born and raised in Dagenham, Essex, England. She attended Robert Clack Technical School in Becontree Heath, Dagenham. After leaving school, she worked at the Ford Dagenham factory and also engaged in part-time modelling. Her singing talents emerged when she secured the second position in a local talent contest. Her potential caught the attention of singer Adam Faith, who introduced her to his manager, Eve Taylor. Under Taylor's guidance, Sandie Shaw signed a contract with Pye Records in 1964 and adopted the stage name 'Sandie Shaw.'

Collaborating with songwriter Chris Andrews, Shaw released her first single, "As Long as You're Happy Baby," followed by "(There's) Always Something There to Remind Me." The latter song, originally by Burt Bacharach and Hal David, became a UK chart-topper in 1964. Shaw's popularity soared with hits like "Girl Don't Come," "I'll Stop at Nothing," "Long Live Love," and "Message Understood." She also embraced diverse languages, recording versions of her songs in Italian, French, German, and Spanish, expanding her fanbase across Europe.

After a period of declining record sales in the late 1960s, Shaw ventured into cabaret performances. Her influence extended beyond music as she became a committed practitioner of Sōka Gakkai Buddhism and pursued academic studies in psychotherapy. In the 1980s, her collaboration with contemporary artists and a renewed interest in recording revitalised her career. She worked with the Smiths, reinterpreting some of their songs, and continued to perform on various platforms.

Shaw's journey in the 1990s and early 2000s encompassed a range of activities, including music releases, writing, and her involvement in psychological healthcare through her Arts Clinic. Her impact was acknowledged with appointments and awards, including becoming a Member of the Order of the British Empire (MBE) in 2017. Throughout her career, Shaw exhibited resilience, versatility, and a dedication to creative expression that left an indelible mark on the music and cultural landscape.

Shaw's personal life involved multiple marriages, including unions with fashion designer Jeff Banks, Nik Powell (co-founder of the Virgin Group), and psychologist Tony Bedford. She balanced her music career with her roles as a mother and wife.

Beyond her artistic pursuits, Shaw has expressed her views on human rights issues and politics. She lent her voice to campaigns by Amnesty International and shared her opinions on topics such as the Scottish independence referendum and the

European Union. Her influence extended beyond the stage, showcasing her commitment to social causes and her engagement in public discourse.

Puppet on a String was crafted by the songwriting duo Bill Martin and Phil Coulter.

Upon its release as Shaw's thirteenth UK single, the track soared to the top of the UK Singles Chart on 27th April 1967. It maintained its prime position for three consecutive weeks. Beyond the UK, the song achieved recognition in the United States, where Al Hirt's 1967 rendition reached No.18 on the Adult Contemporary chart and No.129 on the Billboard Hot 100.

Sandie Shaw's journey with "Puppet on a String" began when she performed it as one of five potential contenders to represent the United Kingdom in the Eurovision Song Contest 1967 on The Rolf Harris Show. Despite initial hesitations, Shaw's manager, Adam Faith, persuaded her to participate, considering it a prudent career move. This decision was driven by the desire to enhance her cabaret appeal and her public image.

Among the five showcased songs, "Puppet on a String" was the one that Shaw held least dear. She admitted to having a strong aversion to the song's melody and what she perceived as its sexist lyrics. Despite her reservations, the song was selected as her Eurovision entry and ultimately clinched victory. It is worth noting that her popularity across Europe played a role in her triumph, as she had previously recorded many of her hit singles in multiple languages, broadening her appeal.

In response to Shaw's critical assessment of the song, Phil Coulter countered that her analysis might not fully reflect the positive impact the song had on her career. He pointed out that "Puppet on a String" significantly expanded her audience and record sales, even if she had expressed disdain for it over the years. Despite any misgivings, Shaw delivered a commendable performance of the song, leading to her victory. Coulter underscored the song's role in boosting her career beyond the contest.

Shaw's rendition of "Puppet on a String" was not confined to the English language. She showcased her versatility by recording versions of the song in French ("Un tout petit pantin"), Italian ("La danza delle note"), Spanish ("Marionetas en la cuerda"), and German ("Wiedehopf im Mai").

To celebrate her 60th birthday in 2007, Sandie Shaw re-recorded "Puppet on a String." Collaborating with musician Howard Jones, she produced a new version with a slower tempo and electronic elements. The re-recorded version was offered as a free download on her official website for 60 days, garnering popularity and marking a distinctive chapter in her career.

Leaderboard		
Year	Country	Victories
1958, 1960, 1962	France	3
1961, 1965	Luxembourg	2
1957, 1959	Netherlands	2
1967	**United Kingdom**	**1**
1966	Austria	1
1963	Denmark	1
1956	Switzerland	1

Top Scores - 1967				
Country	Artist	Song	Points	Position
United Kingdom	Sandie Shaw	"Puppet on a String"	47	1
Ireland	Sean Dunphy	"If I Could Choose"	22	2

France	Noëlle Cordier	"Il doit faire beau là-bas"	20	3
Luxembourg	Vicky	"L'Amour est bleu"	17	4
Monaco	Minouche Barelli	"Boum-Badaboum"	10	5

1968

The Eurovision Song Contest of 1968 marked the 13th edition of this annual musical extravaganza. This grand event unfolded in **London, United Kingdom**, as a result of the UK's triumph the year before. Surprisingly, even though it was the United Kingdom's maiden victory in 1987, this marked their third time hosting the competition. The UK had previously hosted Eurovision in 1960 and 1963, both times in the vibrant city of London. This splendid gathering, orchestrated by the European Broadcasting Union (EBU) in collaboration with the host broadcaster, the British Broadcasting Corporation (BBC), graced the Royal Albert Hall on the 6th of April 1968. The charming Katie Boyle took on the role of host for the third time, and this edition was historic as it was the first to be broadcast in colour.

A total of **seventeen countries** participated in this musical spectacle, mirroring the lineup from the previous year.

Spain emerged as the victor with the captivating song "**La La La**," performed by **Massiel** and penned by Manuel de la Calva and Ramón Arcusa. This triumph not only secured Spain's first-ever victory in the Eurovision Song Contest but also marked their inaugural placement within the top five contestants.

María de los Ángeles Felisa Santamaría Espinosa, known professionally as Massiel, is a renowned Spanish pop singer. She was born on the 2nd of August 1947.

Massiel was born in Madrid, Spain. Her father, Emilio Santamaria Martín, hailing from Asturias, worked as an artistic manager. Growing up surrounded by singers and musical groups, Massiel's early exposure to the world of music ignited her ambition to become a singer, actress, and songwriter.

Her mother, Concepción Espinosa Peñas (1920-2011), also hailed from Asturias.

Massiel's initial foray into the music industry occurred in 1966 with the release of her first recordings, including songs like "Di que no," "No sé porqué," "Llueve," "No comprendo," "Y sabes qué vi," "Rufo el pescador," "Aleluya," and "El era mi amigo." The song "Rosas en el mar," penned by her friend Luis Eduardo Aute in 1967, catapulted her to fame as a singer in both Spain and Latin America. In 1967, she also ventured into acting with a role in the film "Vestida de novia."

On the 29th of March 1968, Massiel was called upon to replace singer-songwriter Joan Manuel Serrat as Spain's representative at the Eurovision Song Contest. Serrat had intended to perform in Catalan, but the Francoist State insisted on Castilian, in line with its language policies.

Just nine days before the contest, Massiel was on tour in Mexico. She returned to Spain, rapidly learned the song, and recorded it in five languages. On the 6th of April in London, she clinched victory, beating the favourite, Cliff Richard, with "Congratulations" by a single point. Her winning song, "La, la, la," was composed by Ramón Arcusa and Manuel de la Calva. In 2008, a Spanish documentary raised allegations of bribery by Spain's television company TVE, purportedly on orders from General Franco. These claims were based on a statement by journalist José María Íñigo, who later clarified that he had merely repeated a widely circulated rumour, and his words had been taken out of context. Both Massiel and Íñigo accused La Sexta, the channel behind the documentary, of fabricating the scandal.

In the years that followed, Massiel explored dramatic roles in theatrical productions, including "A los hombres futuros," a tribute to Bertolt Brecht (1972), "Corridos de la revolución: Mexico 1910" (1976), and "Antonio and Cleopatra" in the early 1980s.

From 1966 to 1998, Massiel recorded songs spanning various genres for five different record companies: Zafiro, PolyGram, Hispavox, Bat Discos, and Emasstor. Her extensive discography encompasses approximately 50 records, including EPs, singles, LPs, CDs, and compilations. In 1997, she released a Spanish album titled "Baladas Y Canciones De Bertolt Brecht."

Massiel made a notable return in 1981 with a fresh musical direction and signed with a new record label, Hispavox. Her debut under this label, "Tiempos Difíciles," marked a significant comeback in Spain, featuring hit songs like "El Amor" and "Hello America." Her covers of Mexican songs, "Eres" (written by José María Napoleón) and "El Noa Noa" (written by Juan Gabriel), not only introduced Mexican talent to Spain but also gained immense popularity. Massiel continued her resurgence with the 1983 album "Corazon De Hierro," which not only achieved success in her homeland but also rekindled her popularity in Latin America. The song "Brindaremos Por El" from this album became a global hit, topping charts in multiple countries.

During the 1980s, Massiel was invited as a guest artist to the Festival de Viña del Mar in Chile despite the country being under the rule of Augusto Pinochet. Following her performance, she received the festival's most prestigious award, La Gaviota de Plata (The Silver Seagull). In her acceptance speech, she conveyed greetings from Patricio Manns, a well-known composer, poet, and member of the Communist Party of Chile who was in exile in Sweden after the 1973 coup d'état against Salvador Allende.

In 1997, Massiel re-recorded her Eurovision-winning song "La, la, la," infusing it with a 'hip-hop' beat, background singers, whistling, and Spanish percussion. In 1998, she took on the lead role of Maria in the film "Cantando a la Vida," which revolved around a European Song Festival winner who suddenly disappeared. Massiel not only acted in the film but also sang the entire soundtrack.

In 2001, Massiel was involved in an incident when she fell from the window of her second-floor flat while allegedly attempting to close the shutters. In 2005, she made a special appearance on the 50th Anniversary Special of the Eurovision Song Contest, where she performed the song that had made her an international sensation. In 2007, she joined the Mission Eurovision jury, a show dedicated to selecting Spain's entry for the Eurovision Song Contest 2007. This marked her brief return to the music stage after an eleven-year hiatus.

In 2012, Massiel played a starring role in the Spanish production of "Follies" by Stephen Sondheim, directed by Mario Gas. She portrayed the character Carlotta Campion, a former movie star, and delivered the iconic tune "I'm still here." This production ran from February to April at the Teatro Español in Madrid.

La, la, la is a captivating song penned by Manuel de la Calva and Ramón Arcusa.

The performance of "La, la, la" not only secured Spain's first-ever Eurovision win but also marked a historic moment as the first-ever Eurovision Song Contest broadcast in colour. During the performance, viewers noted Massiel's backing singers, who were attired in stylish teal-coloured dresses. These talented singers, from left to right, were María Jesús Aguirre, María Dolores Arenas, and Mercedes Valimaña Macaria.

Massiel's rendition of "La, la, la" was recorded in four languages: Spanish, Italian, and German, all under the title "La, la, la," and in English as "He Gives Me Love (La, la, la)." The song also gained popularity through covers by other artists. Italian singer Mina performed it in Radiotelevisione Italiana's 1968 variety series Canzonissima, and Finnish singer Carola gave her own interpretation. In the United States and Canada, American singer Lesley Gore recorded a version of the song, achieving minor hit status.

The band Saint Etienne also contributed to the song's legacy with another cover version, featured on the album "A Song for Eurotrash" (1998). Their rendition had English lyrics that differed from the original, focusing on the subject of her romantic relationship rather than expressions of gratitude. Notably, Portuguese fado star Amália Rodrigues recorded the most successful version of the song, which was performed in Spanish.

Additionally, Turkish singer Alpay released a Turkish version titled "La La La Şarkı Sözü," which served as the B-side of his 1969 single "Sen Gidince." Other artists who covered the song included Heidi Brühl in German and Marcela Laiferová in Slovak.

Leaderboard		
Year	Country	Victories
1958, 1960, 1962	France	3
1961, 1965	Luxembourg	2
1957, 1959	Netherlands	2
1968	**Spain**	**1**
1967	United Kingdom	1
1966	Austria	1
1963	Denmark	1
1956	Switzerland	1

Country	Artist	Song	Points	Position
Spain	Massiel	"La La La"	29	1
United Kingdom	Cliff Richard	"Congratulations"	28	2
France	Isabelle Aubret	"La Source"	20	3
Ireland	Pat McGeegan	"Chance of a Lifetime"	18	4
Sweden	Claes-Göran Hederström	"Det börjar verka kärlek, banne mej"	15	5

Top Scores - 1968

1969

The 1969 Eurovision Song was held in **Madrid, Spain**. The European Broadcasting Union (EBU) and Spain's Televisión Española (TVE) joined forces to organise this spectacle, which unfolded at the esteemed Teatro Real on 29th March 1969. The delightful Laurita Valenzuela, a Spanish television presenter and actress, had the honour of hosting the event.

Sixteen nations participated in the competition, with Austria opting not to take part that year.

When the final votes were tallied, an unprecedented tie emerged, crowning four countries as joint winners: the **United Kingdom**, represented by Lulu and "Boom Bang-a-Bang"; **Spain**, with Salomé's "Vivo cantando"; the **Netherlands**, featuring Lenny Kuhr and "De troubadour"; and **France**, showcasing Frida Boccara and "Un jour, un enfant." This historic tie had never occurred before in the contest's history. At the time, there were no rules to break such a deadlock, leading to all four nations sharing the victory. This win marked France's fourth, making it the first country to achieve this feat. The Netherlands secured their third win, while Spain and the United Kingdom each notched their second victory. Remarkably, Spain became the first country to clinch back-to-back Eurovision Song Contest wins.

As for the participating countries, Austria's absence from the contest was officially attributed to the inability to find a suitable representative. However, rumours suggested that their decision might have been influenced by the contest's location in Franco-ruled Spain. Additionally, Wales had aspirations to debut in the contest through Welsh language broadcaster BBC Cymru and even held a national selection called Cân i Gymru. Unfortunately, their participation was denied, primarily because Wales is not recognised as a sovereign state, and the exclusive right to represent the United Kingdom at Eurovision belongs to the BBC.

JOINT WINNERS

UNITED KINGDOM

Lulu Kennedy-Cairns CBE, originally born Marie McDonald McLaughlin Lawrie on the 3rd of November 1948, is a renowned Scottish singer, actress, and television personality.

Possessing a commanding singing voice, Lulu began her career in the United Kingdom but quickly gained international recognition. She achieved significant chart success with songs like "To Sir with Love," which featured in the 1967 film of the same name and reached the top of the Billboard Hot 100. She also contributed the title song to the 1974 James Bond film, "The Man with the Golden Gun."

Born in Lennoxtown, Stirlingshire, she grew up in Dennistoun, Glasgow, attending Thomson Street Primary School and Onslow Drive School. At a young age, she showed her singing talent by performing with a band called the Bellrocks. Her manager, Marion Massey, gave her the stage name "Lulu," which means a remarkable or outstanding person. Lulu's family history was explored in the UK series "Who Do You Think You Are?" in August 2017. The research revealed intriguing details, including her maternal grandparents' different religions—her grandfather was a Catholic, while her grandmother was a Protestant. These religious differences led to opposition to their union.

In 1964, at the age of fifteen, Lulu signed with Decca Records and released "Shout," which became a hit in the UK. She toured

Poland with the Hollies in 1966, becoming the first British female singer to perform live behind the Iron Curtain. Lulu later embarked on a solo career and achieved success with songs like "The Boat That I Row."

Lulu made her acting debut in the 1967 film "To Sir, with Love," where she not only acted but also sang the title song. The song became a major hit in the United States, reaching No.1 on the Billboard charts. She also hosted several television series in the late 1960s.

Lulu married Maurice Gibb of the Bee Gees just before her Eurovision appearance in 1969. However, the marriage faced challenges, leading to their divorce in 1973. She later married hairdresser John Frieda, but they divorced in 1991. Lulu and John had one son, Jordan Frieda.

In 1969, Lulu recorded the album "New Routes" at Muscle Shoals studios in Alabama, featuring slide guitarist Duane Allman. In 1974, she performed the title song for the James Bond film "The Man with the Golden Gun." She also covered David Bowie's songs and had a Top 10 hit with "The Man Who Sold the World" in 1974.

Lulu's chart success decreased in the 1980s, but she remained active in various entertainment roles, including acting and hosting a radio show. She co-hosted a revived series of "Oh Boy!" for ITV and won the Rear of the Year award in 1983. Lulu made a comeback in the 1990s, with her single "Independence" reaching No.11 in the UK charts. She also co-wrote the song "I Don't Wanna Fight," which became a hit for Tina Turner. In 2000, Lulu received an OBE from Queen Elizabeth II. She continued to perform and collaborate with artists like Elton John and Paul McCartney. Her autobiography was published in 2002. She toured with Take That in 2019 and has remained active in the entertainment industry.

Lulu has continued to make appearances, including as a guest judge on "RuPaul's Drag Race UK" in 2021. She voiced a character in the film "My Old School" in 2022 and participated in "The Masked Singer" in 2023. Additionally, she embarked on her "For The Record UK Tour" in late 2023, marking her return to live performances.

Boom Bang-a-Bang stands as a notable musical piece penned by Alan Moorhouse and Peter Warne. In terms of lyrics, the song expresses the singer's desire for affection from her lover, imploring them to "cuddle me tight." She goes on to describe how her heart reacts with a rhythmic "boom bang-a-bang" when her beloved is in close proximity, accompanied by corresponding musical notes. "Boom Bang-a-Bang" achieved significant success, reaching the second position on the UK Singles Chart and enjoying widespread popularity across Europe.

Interestingly, more than two decades after its initial release, the song found itself on the BBC's list of banned songs during the 1991 Gulf War. Moreover, "Boom Bang-A-Bang" had the honour of being the title of a one-hour BBC One program created to celebrate the fiftieth anniversary of the Eurovision Song Contest in 2006. Hosted by Sir Terry Wogan and featuring a blend of archived footage and memorable moments from past contests, this special, which aired during the Eurovision week of that year, also included a performance of the UK's entry for that year by Daz Sampson.

Remarkably, "Boom Bang-a-Bang" serves as the theme tune for the BBC Three sitcom "Him & Her," which premiered in 2010.

SPAIN

Maria Rosa Marco Poquet, known by her stage name Salomé, is a prominent Spanish singer, born in Barcelona, Spain, on the 21st of June 1939.

Salomé's career took root in Radio Barcelona, and from there, she embarked on a multifaceted musical journey intertwined with television appearances as a hostess. Her talents even led her to open for the legendary Frank Sinatra. By 1963, Salomé had already recorded an impressive repertoire of over forty songs for esteemed record labels such as Iberofón and Zafiro. In a testament to her prowess, she emerged victorious at the 5th Festival de la Canción Mediterránea de Barcelona music contest in 1963 with her Catalan composition, "Se'n va anar."

Expanding her musical horizons, Salomé clinched the second prize at the 9th Festival de la Canción Mediterránea de Barcelona in 1967 with her Catalan piece titled "Com el vent." Her talents transcended borders as she competed in the Festival de Valencia and the Festival del Duero, where she secured the best singer accolade. In 1969, she celebrated her marriage to Sebastián García.

Salomé's melodic repertoire spanned both Catalan and Spanish languages, featuring hits like "Quinientas millas," "L'arbre," "Bésame mucho," "Com el vent," "L'emigrant," "Puedo morir mañana," "Isla del amor," and "Esperaré."

During the 1969 Eurovision Contest, Salomé was presented with the award by the previous Eurovision victor, the Spanish singer Massiel. Her onstage attire was a creation by the renowned Manuel Pertegaz, featuring a dress weighing 14 kg, adorned with small chalk blue porcelain cylinders and three 1-kg necklaces.

Vivo cantando - The composition of this enchanting piece is credited to María José de Cerato and Aniano Alcalde, with production helmed by Augusto Algueró.

The essence of "Vivo cantando" is a vivacious and up-tempo melody delivered from the perspective of a woman expressing the profound positive impact her lover has had on her life. The central theme revolves around her newfound joy in living a life filled with song.

Salomé's rendition of this remarkable song transcended linguistic boundaries, as she recorded it in six languages: Spanish (Castilian), Catalan (titled as "Canto i vull viure"), Basque ("Kantari bizi naiz"), English ("The Feeling of Love"), French ("Alors je chante"), and Italian ("Vivo cantando"). Notably, the French version of the song received a captivating cover by Israeli singer Rika Zaraï, which ascended to the number one spot on the French singles chart, reigning supreme for three weeks from 16th of August to 5th of September 1969. In Spain, the song also claimed the top position on the Spanish Singles Chart.

THE NETHERLANDS

Helena Hubertina Johanna, affectionately known as "Lenny" Kuhr, is a Dutch singer-songwriter born on the 22nd of February 1950.

Lenny Kuhr embarked on her singing career in the Netherlands in 1967, embracing the rich tradition of French chanson in her performances. The early seventies witnessed Kuhr's greater success in France, surpassing her recognition in her home country. In 1970, she joined Georges Brassens on a tour, and in late 1971, she achieved a top 10 hit in France with "Jesus Christo."

A significant milestone in her Dutch career arrived in 1980 with "Visite," her most significant hit in the Netherlands. This song was a collaborative effort with the French group Les Poppys. Lenny Kuhr has continued to release records over the years, although without achieving substantial chart success.

Notably, Lenny Kuhr was among the artists who recorded "Shalom from Holland," a song composed by Simon Hammelburg and Ron Klipstein. This musical gesture of solidarity was dedicated to the Israeli people during the Gulf War in 1991 when they faced the threat of missiles from Iraq.

Returning to the Eurovision stage, Lenny Kuhr graced the interval of the Grand Final of the Eurovision Song Contest on the 22nd of May 2021 in Rotterdam. This special segment, titled "Rock the Roof," featured her performance of "De troubadour" alongside other Eurovision winners.

In her personal life, Lenny Kuhr's first marriage took place in 1974 when she wed an Israeli doctor. They crossed paths after she suffered an attack in May 1973 in Haarlem, which resulted in damage to her nose. Her husband played a crucial role in repairing her nose, and this experience led her to convert to Judaism. The couple welcomed two daughters into the world, one in 1975 and another in 1980. Lenny also spent some time residing in Israel.

Following her divorce, Lenny Kuhr entered a romantic relationship with songwriter Herman Pieter de Boer, a connection that lasted from 1981 to 1993. In 2003, she embarked on a second marriage, marking another chapter in her personal life.

De troubadour is a beautiful blend of musical and lyrical inspiration drawn from folk-song traditions. In her performance,

Kuhr narrates the tale of a troubadour from the Middle Ages, painting a vivid picture of the profound impact his music has on his audiences. Notably, Lenny Kuhr recorded versions of the song in multiple languages, including English ("The Troubadour"), French ("Le troubadour"), German ("Der Troubadour"), Italian ("Un cantastorie"), and Spanish ("El trovador").

Five years after the competition, Kuhr revisited the song with modified Dutch lyrics, renaming it "De generaal" ("The general"). This rendition paid homage to Rinus Michels, the Dutch national soccer coach, who had earned the affectionate nickname "The General" from the Dutch team players.

During the Eurovision event, "De troubadour" was the eighth performance of the night, following the United Kingdom's Lulu with "Boom Bang-a-Bang" and preceding Sweden's Tommy Körberg with "Judy, min vän." When the final votes were tallied, the song had garnered 18 points, securing its place at the top of the leaderboard, tied for first position in a field of 16 competitors. This achievement was particularly remarkable as the Dutch entry in the 1968 contest had finished joint last. Thus, the Netherlands achieved the extraordinary feat of transitioning from the bottom of the rankings to sharing the top spot in the span of just one year.

FRANCE

Danielle Frida Hélène Boccara, born on the 29th of October 1940 in Casablanca, Morocco, was a French singer of Italian heritage who embraced a multilingual repertoire, enchanting audiences with her performances in languages such as French, Spanish, English, Italian, German, Dutch, and Russian.

Boccara's origins are traced back to a Jewish family with Italian roots that had previously resided in Tunisia before settling in

Morocco. At the age of 17, she made a significant move from Casablanca to Paris, France, where her artistic journey as a singer began to flourish. Within her family, talent was abundant, with her brother Jean-Michel Braque (born Roger Boccara) and sister Lina Boccara both making names for themselves in show business. Later, she became a mother to Tristan Boccara, born in the mid-1970s, who followed in her musical footsteps and gained recognition as Goldinski. He also showcased his skills as a composer, pianist, and arranger.

In 1964, Boccara submitted the song "Autrefois" ("In the past") for consideration by the French Eurovision Song Contest selection panel, but she faced disappointment. However, her fortunes changed five years later at the Eurovision Song Contest in 1969, held in Madrid, Spain.

Throughout her career, Eddy Marnay was a significant collaborator, contributing to most of the songs performed by Boccara. Her repertoire also featured works from renowned composers such as Jacques Brel, Georges Brassens, Charles Aznavour, Michel Legrand, Michel Magne, Nino Rota, and Mikis Theodorakis.

Boccara's recording of "Cent mille chansons" ("A hundred thousand songs") in 1968 earned her a gold disc. Following that success, "Un jour, un enfant" (1969) garnered a platinum disc, and "Pour vivre ensemble" ("To live together," 1971) secured another gold. Some of her other famous tracks include "Cherbourg avait raison" (1961), "Aujourd'hui" (1965), "Le moulins de mon cœur" (1969), "L'enfant aux cymbales" (1969), "Belle du Luxembourg" (1969), "La croix, l'étoile et le croissant" (1970), "Venise va mourir" (1970), "Trop jeune ou trop vieux" (1971), "Valdemosa" (1976), "L'année où Piccoli jouait Le choses de la vie" (1978), "Un monde en sarabande" (1979), and "La prière" (1979). In the late 1960s, she also recorded "Un pays pour nous," a French version of "Somewhere" from the musical West Side Story. Leonard Bernstein, the composer of the original melody, declared Boccara's rendition as his favourite.

Boccara maintained her connection to Eurovision by participating in the French national finals of 1980, where she performed "Un enfant de France," and in 1981, with her song "Voilà comment je t'aime." However, neither of these songs was selected for the competition. Tragically, Danielle Frida Hélène Boccara passed away at the age of 55 in Paris, France, in 1996, succumbing to a pulmonary infection after a period of declining health. Her legacy endures through her remarkable contributions to the world of music and her enduring presence in the hearts of her admirers.

Un jour, un enfant is a timeless classical ballad that eloquently captures the wonders of the world from the perspective of a child. Boccara's rendition of this enchanting melody extended beyond French, as she recorded versions in five different languages. These adaptations included English (as "Through the Eyes of a Child"), German ("Es schlägt ein Herz für dich," translated as "A Heart Beats for You"), Spanish ("Un día, un niño," translated as "A Day, a Child"), and Italian ("Canzone di un amore perduto," translated as "Song of a Lost Love").

During the performance at Eurovision, the song graced the stage as the fourteenth act of the evening. It followed Germany's Siw Malmkvist with "Primaballerina" and preceded Portugal's Simone de Oliveira with "Desfolhada portuguesa." As the votes were tallied, "Un jour, un enfant" received 18 points, positioning it in a shared first place in a field of 16 competitors.

Leaderboard

Year	Country	Victories
1958, 1960, 1962, 1969	France	4
1957, 1959, 1969	Netherlands	3
1968, 1969	Spain	2
1967, 1969	United Kingdom	2
1961, 1965	Luxembourg	2
1966	Austria	1
1963	Denmark	1
1956	Switzerland	1

Top Scores - 1969

Country	Artist	Song	Points	Position
Spain	Salomé	"Vivo cantando"	18	1
United Kingdom	Lulu	"Boom Bang-a-Bang"	18	1
Netherlands	Lenny Kuhr	"De troubadour"	18	1
France	Frida Boccara	"Un jour, un enfant"	18	1
Switzerland	Paola	"Bonjour, Bonjour"	13	5
Monaco	Jean Jacques	"Maman, maman"	11	6
Ireland	Muriel Day	"The Wages of Love"	10	7
Belgium	Louis Neefs	"Jennifer Jennings"	10	7

1970

The 1970 Eurovision Song Contest marked the 15th instalment of this annual musical competition, held in **Amsterdam, Netherlands**. It was orchestrated by the European Broadcasting Union (EBU) in collaboration with the Dutch broadcaster Nederlandse Omroep Stichting (NOS). The event unfolded on the 21st of March 1970 within the confines of the RAI Congrescentrum and was charmingly presented by the Dutch television personality Willy Dobbe.

The previous edition had seen four countries share the victory, leading to a conundrum regarding the host nation for 1970. Following Spain's hosting in 1969 and the United Kingdom's turn in 1968, the choice was narrowed down to France and the Netherlands. A ballot was conducted, and the Netherlands was duly selected as the host nation.

In the 1970 edition, a total of **twelve countries** participated, which marked a decrease in numbers compared to previous years, reaching a level last seen in 1959. The decision to reduce participation was attributed to Finland, Norway, Portugal, Sweden, and Austria boycotting the contest. Officially, they cited concerns that the competition favoured larger countries, no longer providing engaging television content. However, there were speculations that this protest was also prompted by the unusual four-way tie result in 1969.

Emerging as the victor in this contest was **Ireland**, with the enchanting song "**All Kinds of Everything**," beautifully performed by **Dana**. This triumph marked Ireland's initial victory out of the eventual seven they would achieve in the competition. The

United Kingdom secured the second position for the seventh time, while Germany secured a commendable third place, their best result at the time. Notably, this event marked the sole instance when Luxembourg received no points.

Dana, originally born as Rosemary Brown in Islington, London, on the 30th of August 1951, was one of seven siblings. Her father, Robert Brown, worked as a porter at King's Cross station in addition to being a barber and trumpeter. Originally hailing from Derry, Northern Ireland, Robert moved the family to London after World War II in search of better job opportunities. When Dana was five, the family relocated to Derry, where she grew up in the Creggan housing estate and Bogside.

At the young age of six, Dana won her first talent contest, and her nickname "Dana" (Irish for bold or mischievous) was coined by other children in her community due to her interest in practising judo moves. She later attended Thornhill College, a girls' Catholic school in Derry. At the age of 14, she worked a summer job at the Bazooka chewing gum factory in Essex.

Shortly before turning 16, Dana signed with Rex Records, a subsidiary of Decca Records, with the assistance of her teacher and music promoter, Tony Johnston. Performing under the name Dana, she debuted with the single "Sixteen," written by Tony Johnston, and "Little Girl Blue" on the B-side, which was her own composition. While studying A-level music and English, she gained popularity in Dublin's cabaret and folk clubs during the weekends and was crowned Queen of Cabaret at Clontarf Castle in 1968. She was encouraged to audition for the Irish National Song Contest, where she sang "Look Around" by Michael Reade during the final, finishing second to Muriel Day and "Wages of Love."

In December 1969, Tom McGrath, the producer of the Irish National Song Contest, invited Dana to participate again the following year, believing that the ballad "All Kinds of Everything" would be a suitable song for her. Dana's second attempt at winning the Irish contest proved successful.

Dana's debut album, "All Kinds of Everything," was recorded at Decca Studios in West Hampstead, London, in April 1970 and included four tracks co-written by Dana herself, along with a new recording of the album's title track. Her follow-up single, "I Will Follow You," was released in September but failed to chart significantly.

A turning point in her career came with the release of "Who Put the Lights Out," written by Paul Ryan for his twin brother. Dana's version of the song, produced by Bill Landis, became a hit in Ireland and reached No.14 in the UK in March 1971. She continued to release singles, including "Sunday Monday Tuesday," which reached No.4 in the Irish chart in December 1973. However, her success waned in the subsequent years.

To revive her career, Dana joined GTO Records and released "Please Tell Him That I Said Hello" in 1974, which reached No.7 in Ireland and later charted in the UK. She recorded foreign-language versions of songs, including "Wenn ein Mädchen verliebt ist" (German, 1971), "Tu Me Dis I Love You" (French, 1975), and a Japanese version of "It's Gonna be a Cold Cold Christmas" in 1976.

Her single "It's Gonna be a Cold Cold Christmas" in 1975 became her biggest international success since her Eurovision victory. It reached No.4 in the UK and garnered awards for Best Female Singer from the NME and TV Times in the UK at the end of the year.

In September 1976, while promoting her single "Fairytale," Dana lost her voice due to vocal cord issues. She underwent surgery to remove a non-malignant growth from her left vocal cord and a small part of the cord itself. Despite concerns that she might never sing again, Dana resumed live performances in December 1977 with the help of a vocal coach.

In the late 1970s, Barry Blue produced her fifth album, "The Girl is Back," which was released in April 1979. The album contained no cover versions and featured the track "Something's Cookin' in the Kitchen" by Dave Jordan, which became her only UK hit single from the album, reaching No.44.

In January 1980, Dana achieved an Irish number one with the song "Totus Tuus," inspired by Pope John Paul II's motto. This marked the beginning of her association with Christian music, and she soon found a significant audience in the American Christian market. Her album "Everything is Beautiful" in late 1980, subtitled "20 Inspirational Songs," became her biggest-selling album in the UK, reaching No.43 in the chart in January 1981. Dana released her first Christian album for Word Records later that year, titled "Totally Yours," featuring songs like "Praise the Lord," "The Soft Rain," and "Totus Tuus," credited to "Dana and Damien Scallon." Another song, "Little Baby (Grace's Song)," was written during her pregnancy with their first child.

In 1982, Dana recorded the pop album "Magic" for Lite Records, which included songs written by her younger brothers, John and Gerald Brown, along with the single "I Feel Love Comin' On," written by Barry White. Dana's second album for Word Records, "Let There Be Love," showcased up-tempo Christian pop, jazz, ballads, and an old Irish hymn sung in Gaelic called "Ag Criost an Siol."

She also took on the role of Snow White in a West End production of "Snow White and the Seven Dwarfs" during the 1983 Christmas and New Year pantomime season, setting box-office records.

Dana toured the United States in 1984 to promote her Word albums, performing in concert halls, churches, colleges, and on TV and radio. In 1985, Hodder and Stoughton published her autobiography, "Dana – An Autobiography," which covered her childhood, married life, music career, and growing devotion to God. She also released a fifties tribute album titled "If I Give My Heart to You" in 1985.

In June 1997, Dana received a letter from the Christian Community Centre in Ireland suggesting that she run for the presidency of Ireland. Initially uninterested in politics and unfamiliar with the organisation, she eventually decided to seek nomination as an independent candidate in the 1997 Irish presidential election under the name Dana Rosemary Scallon. Her campaign focused on protecting the Irish Constitution and required amending it through a public ballot. She became the first-ever presidential candidate to secure a nomination solely from County and City Councils.

Although she did not win the presidency, Dana Rosemary Scallon received 175,458 of the first-preference votes (13.8%), coming third to Fianna Fáil's candidate and eventual winner, Mary McAleese.

In 1999, Dana was granted US citizenship, renouncing allegiance to any other state. That same year, she won a seat as an independent candidate in the European Parliament, representing Connacht–Ulster. Her campaign centred on family values and her strong anti-abortion stance, opposing abortion in all cases.

Throughout her political career, Dana remained opposed to divorce and same-sex marriage and held Eurosceptic views on the EU. Despite several approaches from Fianna Fáil, she chose not to associate with any political party. Her MEP term marked the end of her eight-year stay in the US.

In the early 2000s, Dana continued her involvement in entertainment by participating in TV shows like "The All Ireland Talent Show" in 2009 and the "Best of British Variety" tour in 2010. She also appeared as a contestant on the fourth series of the reality television program "Celebrity Bainisteoir" in 2011 but had to withdraw when she announced her candidacy for the Irish presidency once again.

During the campaign, she emphasised her commitment to protecting Irish sovereignty and the need for a public ballot to amend the Irish Constitution. However, she faced criticism for her statements, as the President does not possess veto power over bills but can refer them to the Council of State for consideration.

Scallon's dual US and Irish citizenship came to light during the campaign, but she stated that it was not a significant issue. In a debate on Prime Time, she addressed a "malicious" accusation made against her and her family in the US, vowing to pursue the responsible parties. This incident garnered media attention. Ultimately, Dana received 51,220 votes (2.9%) in the 2011 election, finishing in sixth place behind the eventual winner, Michael D. Higgins.

In 2019, Dana announced her return to the studio to record a new album. She promoted her single "Falling" on various television and radio shows, and her album titled "My Time" was released on 1st November 2019. In 2023, Dana released a new version of her hit song 'Fairytale' and conducted a series of interviews on UTV Live, Good Morning Britain, and GB News.

All Kinds of Everything is a charming song penned by the talented songwriters Derry Lindsay and Jackie Smith. Dana's lyrics convey a poignant message as she sings about various everyday things that remind her of her sweetheart, including wishing wells, wedding bells, and the morning dew. Each verse concludes with the heartfelt admission that "all kinds of everything remind me of you." Dana's rendition of this song resonated with audiences across the globe, making it an international hit.

Dana's song, "All Kinds of Everything," was the brainchild of Derry Lindsay and Jackie Smith, two amateur songwriters working as compositors for a Dublin newspaper. The song's publishing rights were held by Scottish songwriter Bill Martin, who claimed authorship along with his songwriting partner Phil Coulter. However, it is worth noting that this claim was contested, and Derry Lindsay later clarified the true authors of the song in an interview with The Irish Times.

"All Kinds of Everything" also achieved commercial success, reaching No.1 on the charts in Ireland even before its Eurovision win. In the UK, it topped the charts for two weeks in April 1970. The song also enjoyed chart success in several other countries, including the Netherlands, Austria, Belgium, New Zealand, South Africa, Switzerland, and West Germany.

In Australia, Dana's version faced competition from a cover by Pat Carroll, which reached No.25 on the charts. Interestingly, the joint ranking of both versions reached No.34.

The overall sales of Dana's "All Kinds of Everything" are estimated to have reached an impressive two million units. Interestingly, the song found a place in the 2011 movie "Tinker Tailor Soldier Spy."

Leaderboard		
Year	Country	Victories
1958, 1960, 1962, 1969	France	4
1957, 1959, 1969	Netherlands	3
1968, 1969	Spain	2
1967, 1969	United Kingdom	2
1961, 1965	Luxembourg	2
1970	**Ireland**	**1**
1966	Austria	1
1963	Denmark	1
1956	Switzerland	1

Top Scores - 1970				
Country	Artist	Song	Points	Position
Ireland	Dana	"All Kinds of Everything"	32	1
United Kingdom	Mary Hopkin	"Knock, Knock (Who's There?)"	26	2
Germany	Katja Ebstein	"Wunder gibt es immer wieder"	12	3
Switzerland	Henri Dès	"Retour"	8	4
France	Guy Bonnet	"Marie-Blanche"	8	4
Spain	Julio Iglesias	"Gwendolyne"	8	4

1971

The 1971 Eurovision Song Contest marked the 16th instalment of this annual event. **Dublin, Ireland**, served as the host city, chosen due to Ireland's victory the previous year. The European Broadcasting Union (EBU) and host broadcaster Radio Telefís Éireann (RTÉ) orchestrated the competition, which unfolded at the Gaiety Theatre on 3rd April 1971. The charismatic Irish television presenter Bernadette Ní Ghallchóir took on the role of the host.

A total of **eighteen countries** participated in this edition, matching the record set in 1965 and 1966. Austria made a comeback after a two-year absence, while Finland, Norway, Portugal, and Sweden returned to the competition after boycotting the previous year's event. Notably, Malta made its debut appearance in the contest.

Monaco emerged as the victor with the enchanting song "**Un banc, un arbre, une rue**," performed by **Séverine**. Monaco's triumph in 1971 marked their first and only victory in the history of the Eurovision Song Contest. Additionally, this unique edition of the competition saw the second and third-placed entrants also receiving recognition, a departure from the norm.

Séverine, born Josiane Grizeau on the 10th of October 1948, is a renowned French vocalist who etched her name in the annals of music history by securing victory in the Eurovision Song Contest in 1971. Séverine's determination to conquer the Eurovision stage did not wane after her initial triumph. She made two subsequent attempts to clinch victory in the Eurovision Song Contest, first participating in the German national finals in 1975 and then returning for another shot in 1982.

In addition to her musical career, Séverine has demonstrated her talent in the world of cinema. She is known for her roles in notable films such as "Rider on the Rain" (1970), "Du soleil plein les yeux" (1970) and appearances on television shows like "Die Drehscheibe" (1964).

Un banc, un arbre, une rue (translated as "A Bench, a Tree, a Street") is a timeless French ballad characterised by heartfelt lyrics that delve into the themes of lost childhood innocence and the pursuit of dreams. The opening lines of the chorus resonate with the sentiment: "we all have a bench, a tree, a street / Where we cherished our dreams / a childhood that has been too short."

During the Eurovision performance, Séverine was accompanied by four teenage male backup singers. In the lead-up to the event, she performed the song in the tranquil setting of Monte Carlo's square. Her performance included a poignant moment where she walked to a bench, sat down during the middle verses, and concluded the song by walking out of the camera's focus.

"Un banc, un arbre, une rue" took the stage as the third performance of the night, following Malta's Joe Grech with "Marija l-Maltija" and preceding Switzerland's Peter, Sue & Marc with "Les illusions de nos vingt ans." When the voting concluded, it had amassed a total of 128 points, securing the top position among 18 competing entries.

Séverine's rendition of the song was not confined to French; she recorded it in four languages, including English (as "Chance in Time"), German ("Mach' die Augen zu (und wünsch dir einen Traum)"), and Italian ("Il posto"). Interestingly, despite the availability of an English version, the original French rendition made its mark by reaching the UK Top 10—a remarkable achievement for a non-Anglophone song in that market.

In addition to Séverine's recordings, Paul Mauriat created an instrumental version of the song for his 1971 LP, also titled "Un banc, un arbre, une rue." This instrumental rendition became the theme tune for the Miss Hong Kong Pageant in 1973, becoming a beloved tune among generations of Hong Kong residents. Furthermore, various artists, including Carola Standertskjöld in Finnish ("Penkki, puu ja puistotie"), Siw Malmkvist in Swedish ("På en gammal bänk" or "On an old bench"), Kirsti Sparboe in Norwegian ("På en gammel benk" or "On an old bench"), and Heli Lääts and Liilia Vahtramäe in Estonian ("Tänav, pink ja puu" or "A Street, a Bench and a Tree"), contributed their interpretations of this enchanting song in their respective languages.

Leaderboard		
Year	Country	Victories
1958, 1960, 1962, 1969	France	4
1957, 1959, 1969	Netherlands	3
1968, 1969	Spain	2
1967, 1969	United Kingdom	2
1961, 1965	Luxembourg	2
1971	**Monaco**	**1**
1970	Ireland	1
1966	Austria	1
1963	Denmark	1
1956	Switzerland	1

Top Scores - 1971				
Country	Artist	Song	Points	Position
Monaco	Séverine	"Un banc, un arbre, une rue"	128	1
Spain	Karina	"En un mundo nuevo"	116	2
Germany	Katja Ebstein	"Diese Welt"	100	3
United Kingdom	Clodagh Rodgers	"Jack in the Box"	98	4
Italy	Massimo Ranieri	"L'amore è un attimo"	91	5

1972

The 17th edition of the Eurovision Song Contest took place in **Edinburgh, United Kingdom**, organised by the European Broadcasting Union (EBU) and hosted by the British Broadcasting Corporation (BBC); the event was held at the Usher Hall on the 25th of March 1972. Moira Shearer, a Scottish ballet dancer, hosted the contest.

The decision to host the event in the UK came after Monaco, the winner of the 1971 contest, was unable to fulfil the hosting requirements and find a suitable venue. **Eighteen countries** participated, the same number as the previous year. **Luxembourg** emerged as the winner with the song "**Après toi**," performed by **Vicky Leandros**. "Après toi" secured victory with the lowest percentage of the total vote, garnering just 8.30% of the available points. Germany secured the third-place finish for the third consecutive year, matching their highest placement from the two previous editions.

Vicky Leandros, born Vasiliki Papathanasiou on the 23rd of August 1949, is a Greek singer residing in Germany. She is the daughter of the renowned singer, musician, and composer Leandros Papathanasiou, also known as Leo Leandros and Mario Panas. In 1967, she gained global recognition by securing fourth place for Luxembourg in the Eurovision Song Contest with the song "L'amour est bleu," which became a worldwide hit. Her career reached new heights when she won the Eurovision Song Contest in 1972.

Beyond her musical success, Vicky Leandros ventured into Greek politics, becoming a town councillor of Piraeus in 2006. However, she later resigned in 2008, citing the challenge of balancing political duties with her singing career.

Early in her career, Leandros showcased her talent in multiple languages, releasing albums and singles worldwide. She hosted a TV show called "Ich Bin" in 1970, which received acclaim for its originality.

Throughout the 1970s, Leandros continued to produce hits, such as "O Kaymos" and "When Bouzoukis Played." She found success in various countries, including Germany and South Africa. In the 1980s, she experienced a comeback with albums like "Verlorenes Paradies" and "Eine Nacht in Griechenland."

The 1990s saw Vicky Leandros enjoying success in Greece and Germany with albums like "Prosexe" and singles like "Du Bist Mein Schönster Gedanke." Collaborating with hitmaker Jack White, she achieved high-charting records.

In the 2000s, Leandros took on the role of a producer, releasing successful albums like "Jetzt / Now." She collaborated with artists like Chris De Burgh and gained chart success in various countries. Her career continued with the 2010 album "Zeitlos," featuring French songs and world hits in the German language. Notably, in 2011, she collaborated with Scooter on the single "C'est Bleu."

In her personal life, Vicky Leandros was married to Greek entrepreneur Ivan Zissiadis from 1982 to 1986 and later to Enno von Ruffin from May 1986 to 2005. The couple had two daughters, Maximiliane and Alessandra. Throughout her illustrious career, Vicky Leandros received numerous awards, including the "Bronze Rose of Montreux," "Goldene Europa," "Record Award of USA," and "Song Statue of Japan."

Après toi was the creation of Leandros' father, Leandros Papathanasiou, also known as Leo Leandros, under his pseudonym Mario Panas. "Après toi" is a poignant ballad, with the singer narrating the impact on her life once her lover has left her for someone else; "After you, I will be nothing but the shadow of your shadow."

The song took the stage as the seventeenth performance of the night (following Belgium's Serge & Christine Ghisoland with "À la folie ou pas du tout" and preceding the Netherlands' Sandra & Andres with "Als het om de liefde gaat"). When the votes were tallied, it garnered 128 points, securing the top position among 18 contestants.

Originally composed with German lyrics ("Dann kamst du"), the song was initially submitted for the German Eurovision national selection process. After not qualifying for that competition, Yves Dessca, co-writer of the lyrics for the 1971 winning song "Un banc, un arbre, une rue," penned French lyrics. The song was then internally selected to represent Luxembourg.

Vicky Leandros also recorded the song in English as "Come What May," achieving widespread release globally. In South Africa, it secured a number one position, while in the United Kingdom and Ireland, it reached the second spot in both charts. Leandros also recorded versions in Italian ("Dopo te"), German ("Dann kamst du"), Spanish ("Y después"), Greek ("Móno esý," Μόνο εσύ), and Japanese ("Omoide ni ikiru," 思い出に生きる).

The English version, "Come What May," found a cover by Filipina singer Pilita Corrales on her 1976 album "Live At The Riviera With Pilita Amado Vol. 2."

Leaderboard

Year	Country	Victories
1958, 1960, 1962, 1969	France	4
1957, 1959, 1969	Netherlands	3
1961, 1965, 1972	**Luxembourg**	**3**
1968, 1969	Spain	2
1967, 1969	United Kingdom	2
1971	Monaco	1
1970	Ireland	1
1966	Austria	1
1963	Denmark	1
1956	Switzerland	1

Top Scores - 1972

Country	Artist	Song	Points	Position
Luxembourg	Vicky Leandros	"Après toi"	128	1
United Kingdom	The New Seekers	"Beg, Steal or Borrow"	114	2
Germany	Mary Roos	"Nur die Liebe läßt uns leben"	107	3
Netherlands	Sandra and Andres	"Als het om de liefde gaat"	106	4
Austria	The Milestones	"Falter im Wind"	100	5

1973

The 1973 Eurovision Song Contest marked its 18th edition, hosted in **Luxembourg City, Luxembourg**. The event unfolded at the Grand Théâtre on 7th April 1973 and was orchestrated by the European Broadcasting Union (EBU) in collaboration with the host broadcaster, Compagnie Luxembourgeoise de Télédiffusion (CLT).

Seventeen countries participated in the competition, with Austria and Malta abstaining, while Israel made its debut appearance. German television host Helga Guitton presented the event.

Luxembourg achieved a consecutive victory with the song "**Tu te reconnaîtras**" by **Anne-Marie David**. The voting process was closely contested, with Spain's entry, "Eres tú" by Mocedades, trailing by just 4 points. The United Kingdom, represented by "Power to All Our Friends" by Cliff Richard (who had previously secured second place in 1968, just behind Spain), followed closely with an additional 2 points. The winning song set a record, scoring the highest points ever achieved in Eurovision under any voting format until 1975. It garnered 129 points out of a possible 160, constituting almost 81% of the maximum score. This accomplishment was partly attributed to a scoring system ensuring that each country received at least two points from every other participating country.

Anne-Marie David (born 23rd May 1952) is a French singer whose musical journey began at the age of 18 in Paris, where she delved into the world of musical theatre. In 1972, she took on the role of Mary Magdalene in the French production of Jesus Christ

Superstar. During the same year, she submitted the song "Un peu romantique" to the French Eurovision Song Contest selection committee, earning a spot in the final shortlist of ten songs.

Following her Eurovision success, Anne-Marie embarked on a global tour, spending a period of time living in Turkey, where she recorded singles in Turkish and received acclaim. Her return to Eurovision in 1979 saw her representing France with the song "Je suis l'enfant soleil," resulting in another closely contested finish, with Israel's "Hallelujah" claiming victory.

Anne-Marie's musical journey continued with tours in France in the 1980s, a period spent in Norway between 1982 and 1983, and a temporary retirement from music in 1987. She made a comeback in 2003, gracing the stage at the 50th anniversary festival of the Eurovision Song Contest in Copenhagen, where she performed her 1972 winning song, "Après toi."

In 2011, Anne-Marie released a revamped version of her 1973-winning song, titled "Tu Te Reconnaîtras (Encore Une Fois)." Collaborating with German pop artist Mave O'Rick in 2015, she released the comeback single "International," recommended for nomination in the Eurovision Song Contest 2016.

A unique chapter in Anne-Marie's story unfolded in 2017 when, after a chance meeting in Austria, she discovered the story of King Edmund, the first patron saint of the English. Inspired, she collaborated with composer Jean Musy to create an Oratorio musical based on the legend of King Edmund. The Oratorio was performed in Boulogne-sur-mer and Amboise, France, with plans for a full English version in St Mary's Church in November 2024. The project faced delays during the COVID lockdown years but regained momentum in 2023.

Tu te reconnaîtras (You'll Recognise Yourself) took to the Eurovision stage as the eleventh performer of the night, following Italy's Massimo Ranieri with "Chi sarà con te" and preceding Sweden's Nova with "You're Summer."

Notably, "Tu te reconnaîtras" is the sole winning entry for Luxembourg with some degree of local involvement. While Anne-Marie David, composer Claude Morgan, and lyricist Vline Buggy were all French, the conductor Pierre Cao hailed from Luxembourg.

Anne-Marie David recorded her winning entry in five languages: French, English ("Wonderful Dream"), German (as "Du bist da"), Spanish ("Te reconocerás"), and uniquely, two entirely different Italian translations titled "Il letto del re" ("The King's Bed") and "Non si vive di paura" ("You Can't Live By Fear") respectively.

In 1973, Turkish pop singer Nilüfer Yumlu released a Turkish-language version of the song titled "Göreceksin kendini," which achieved considerable success in Turkey. Additionally, Finnish singer Katri Helena presented a Finnish-language version, "Nuoruus on seikkailu" ("Being Young is an Adventure"). Czech singer Věra Špinarová contributed a Czech-language version, "Zpívej jak já" ("Sing like me"). Polish singer Irena Jarocka also released a Polish-language rendition, "Ty i ja – wczoraj i dziś" ("You and I – Yesterday and Today").

Leaderboard		
Year	Country	Victories
1961, 1965, 1972, 1973	Luxembourg	4
1958, 1960, 1962, 1969	France	4
1957, 1959, 1969	Netherlands	3
1968, 1969	Spain	2
1967, 1969	United Kingdom	2

1971	Monaco	1
1970	Ireland	1
1966	Austria	1
1963	Denmark	1
1956	Switzerland	1

Top Scores - 1973				
Country	Artist	Song	Points	Position
Luxembourg	Anne-Marie David	"Tu te reconnaîtras"	129	1
Spain	Mocedades	"Eres tú"	125	2
United Kingdom	Cliff Richard	"Power to All Our Friends"	123	3
Israel	Ilanit	"Ey Sham"	97	4
Sweden	The Nova	"You're Summer"	94	5

1974

The 1974 Eurovision Song Contest marked the 19th edition, hosted in **Brighton, United Kingdom**. Organised by the European Broadcasting Union (EBU) and the host broadcaster British Broadcasting Corporation (BBC), the UK took on the hosting responsibilities after Luxembourg, winner of the 1972 and 1973 contests, declined due to financial reasons. The contest unfolded at the Brighton Dome on 6th April 1974, with Katie Boyle serving as the host for the fourth and final time, having previously hosted the 1960, 1963, and 1968 editions.

Seventeen countries participated in the event, with the notable absence of France and the debut of Greece in the competition. The winning entry was "**Waterloo**," performed by **ABBA**, representing **Sweden**. ABBA went on to become one of the best-selling acts in the history of pop music.

France withdrew during the contest week due to the sudden death of President Georges Pompidou. Given the memorial service for President Pompidou, held on the same day as the contest and attended by international dignitaries, it was deemed inappropriate for France to participate. France, originally scheduled to perform the fourteenth, did not present their song "La Vie à vingt-cinq ans," written by Christine Fontaine and intended to be performed by Dani, with Jean-Claude Petit conducting the orchestra. Dani was seen by the audience at the point where the French song should have been performed.

ABBA was formed in Stockholm in 1972; its members include Agnetha Fältskog, Björn Ulvaeus, Benny Andersson, and Anni-Frid Lyngstad. The group's name cleverly incorporates the initials of each member's first name in a palindromic fashion. ABBA has earned its place as one of the most revered and successful musical acts in history, reigning over global charts from 1974 to 1982 and making a triumphant return in 2022.

In 1974, ABBA secured Sweden's first victory in the Eurovision Song Contest with the iconic "Waterloo," later recognised as the best song in the competition's history during its 50th-anniversary celebration in 2005. The group's active years were marked by the collaboration of two married couples—Fältskog and Ulvaeus, and Lyngstad and Andersson. As their fame soared, personal challenges led to the dissolution of both marriages, a shift reflected in the group's later compositions, featuring more introspective and sombre lyrics.

Following their disbandment in December 1982, Andersson and Ulvaeus continued to thrive, crafting music for various mediums, including stage productions, musicals, and movies. Meanwhile, Fältskog and Lyngstad pursued successful solo careers. A decade after their separation, the compilation "ABBA Gold" emerged as a global best-seller in 1992. In 1999, their music found a new life in "Mamma Mia!," a stage musical that achieved worldwide success and remains one of the top-ten longest-running productions on both Broadway and the West End.

ABBA's influence extended to the big screen with the release of the film "Mamma Mia!" in 2008, becoming the highest-grossing film in the United Kingdom that year. The sequel, "Mamma Mia! Here We Go Again," followed in 2018. In 2016, the group reunited to embark on a digital avatar concert tour, and in 2021, they released "Voyage," their first studio album in 40 years, receiving positive critical acclaim and robust sales worldwide. The innovative concert residency, ABBA Voyage, featuring virtual avatars of the group, opened in London in May 2022.

ABBA gained widespread recognition not only for their musical prowess but also for their vibrant and trend-setting costumes. The eccentric outfits were not merely a fashion statement but had a practical origin rooted in Swedish tax law. The cost of the flamboyant attire was tax-deductible, provided that these garments were exclusively reserved for performances.

In the early years, Anni-Frid Lyngstad took on the role of a designer, personally crafting and sewing the outfits. As the group's success surged, they enlisted the expertise of professional theatrical clothes designer Owe Sandström and tailor Lars Wigenius. Lyngstad remained actively involved, suggesting ideas and ensuring that the costumes harmonised with the concert set designs. Graham Tainton's choreography further enhanced their distinctive performance style.

The videos accompanying ABBA's chart-topping hits are often considered pioneering examples of the genre. Directed primarily by Lasse Hallström, known for later directing acclaimed films such as "My Life as a Dog," "The Cider House Rules," and "Chocolat," these videos and the film "ABBA: The Movie" played a crucial role in shaping early visual storytelling in music.

The decision to create videos stemmed from the band's international success, making personal appearances challenging in every country. The strategy also aimed to reduce the need for extensive travel, especially to destinations requiring long flights. Agnetha Fältskog and Björn Ulvaeus, with young children in tow, faced the additional hurdle of Fältskog's fear of flying. ABBA's manager, Stig Anderson, recognised the potential of using video clips to publicise their singles or albums quickly and efficiently, offering broader exposure than traditional concert tours. Many of these videos have since become iconic, characterised by

1970s-era costumes and early video effects, such as unique pairings of band members and creative overlays of faces.

ABBA's impact on the music industry is staggering, with estimated record sales ranging from 150 million to 385 million worldwide. They hold the distinction of being the 3rd best-selling singles artist in the United Kingdom, with 11.3 million singles sold by November 2012. In May 2023, ABBA was honoured with the BRIT Billion Award, recognising their achievement of surpassing one billion UK streams in their career.

As pioneers from a non-English-speaking country, ABBA achieved consistent success in English-speaking charts across the globe, including the United Kingdom, Australia, the United States, the Republic of Ireland, Canada, New Zealand, and South Africa. They are the best-selling Swedish band of all time and the top-selling band originating in continental Europe. ABBA's remarkable journey includes eight consecutive number-one albums in the UK and significant success in Latin America, where they recorded a collection of their hit songs in Spanish.

The group's contributions have earned them a place in the Vocal Group Hall of Fame in 2002 and the prestigious Rock and Roll Hall of Fame in 2010. In 2015, their timeless anthem "Dancing Queen" was inducted into the Recording Academy's Grammy Hall of Fame, solidifying ABBA's enduring impact on the world of music.

Waterloo stands as the inaugural single from ABBA's second album of the same name, marking their debut under the Atlantic label in the US and the first to bear the name ABBA as the performing group. The title and lyrics draw inspiration from the historic 1815 Battle of Waterloo, cleverly using it as a metaphor for a romantic relationship. The Swedish release of the single featured the Swedish version of "Honey, Honey," while the English version included "Watch Out" as the B-side.

In 2005, during the Eurovision Song Contest's 50th-anniversary celebration, "Waterloo" was unanimously chosen as the best song in the competition's history. This accolade was reiterated in 2021 through a 14-country open vote leading up to the Eurovision Song Contest, where it triumphed over Sweden's subsequent winning songs in 2012 and 2015.

The song's creation was purposeful, tailored for entry into the 1974 Eurovision Song Contest following ABBA's third-place finish with "Ring Ring" in the previous year's Swedish pre-selection contest. Originally titled "Honey Pie," "Waterloo" embraced a distinctive blend of rock and jazz beats, a departure from the typical ABBA sound.

Recorded in December 1973, with contributions from Janne Schaffer, Rutger Gunnarsson, and Ola Brunkert, the song's production drew inspiration from Phil Spector's "Wall of Sound." The influence of Spector's layered instrumental overdubs became a defining element of ABBA's musical style. Additionally, German and French versions were recorded in March and April 1974, with the French adaptation undertaken by Alain Boublil, later known for co-writing the musical "Les Misérables."

The lyrics of "Waterloo" use metaphorical language to narrate a woman's surrender to love, drawing parallels to Napoleon's defeat at the Battle of Waterloo in 1815.

ABBA considered submitting another song, "Hasta Mañana," to Eurovision but opted for "Waterloo" to showcase the talents of both lead vocalists, Agnetha Fältskog and Anni-Frid Lyngstad. The performance at Melodifestivalen 1974, sung in Swedish, won and propelled the song to Eurovision victory.

Waterloo broke the Eurovision tradition of dramatic ballads with its lively rhythm, flashy costumes (including silver platform boots), and simple choreography, capturing the audience's attention. Notably, it was the first winning entry in a language other than that of the home country, owing to a temporary lifting of language restrictions between 1973 and 1976.

Scoring 24 points, "Waterloo" clinched victory in the Eurovision Song Contest 1974, surpassing Italy's entry "Sì" by six points.

The song's reception extended beyond Europe, topping charts in the UK for two weeks and becoming ABBA's first of nine UK No. 1 hits. It achieved similar success in numerous countries, including Belgium, Denmark, Finland, West Germany, Ireland, Norway, South Africa, and Switzerland. In the United States, it reached No.6, marking the band's third-highest-charting hit after "Dancing Queen" and "Take a Chance on Me." The song's enduring popularity is evident in its consistent presence among ABBA's top songs in the UK.

Unlike typical Eurovision winners, "Waterloo" transcended geographical boundaries, attaining Top 10 status in Australia, Canada, New Zealand, Rhodesia, and the United States. The accompanying album, "Waterloo," replicated this success in Europe, although it did not match the single's triumph in the US. In retrospect, "Waterloo" remains a solid rock track, securing a lasting place in ABBA's musical legacy and earning admiration for its competent performance and historical narrative.

Leaderboard		
Year	Country	Victories
1961, 1965, 1972, 1973	Luxembourg	4
1958, 1960, 1962, 1969	France	4

1957, 1959, 1969	Netherlands	3
1968, 1969	Spain	2
1967, 1969	United Kingdom	2
1974	**Sweden**	**1**
1971	Monaco	1
1970	Ireland	1
1966	Austria	1
1963	Denmark	1

Top Scores - 1974

Country	Artist	Song	Points	Position
Sweden	ABBA	"Waterloo"	24	1
Italy	Gigliola Cinquetti	"Sì"	18	2
Netherlands	Mouth & MacNeal	"I See a Star"	15	3
United Kingdom	Olivia Newton-John	"Long Live Love"	14	4
Luxembourg	Ireen Sheer	"Bye Bye I Love You"	14	4
Monaco	Romuald	"Celui qui reste et celui qui s'en va"	14	4
Israel	Poogy	"Natati La Khaiai"	11	7
Ireland	Tina Reynolds	"Cross Your Heart"	11	7

1975

The 1975 Eurovision Song Contest marked its 20th edition and was hosted in **Stockholm, Sweden**, organised by the European Broadcasting Union (EBU) and hosted by Sveriges Radio (SR); the event took place at Stockholmsmässan on 22nd of March 1975, with Karin Falck, a Swedish television director, presiding as the host. This occurrence was noteworthy as it was the first time the contest unfolded in Sweden.

A total of **nineteen countries** participated in the competition, surpassing the previous record of eighteen set in 1965. After brief hiatuses, France and Malta returned, and Turkey made its debut. In contrast, Greece abstained following its debut the previous year.

The Netherlands emerged victorious with the song "**Ding-a-dong**," performed by **Teach-In**; this triumph marked the Netherlands' last victory until 2019.

The chosen venue, Stockholmsmässan, situated in Älvsjö, a southern suburb of Stockholm Municipality, accommodated 4,000 people. Constructed in 1971, it served as the backdrop for this significant musical event.

Teach-In, a Dutch band that thrived from 1967 to 1980, gained local prominence in the early 1970s with several top 20 hits in the Netherlands. Throughout their career, the band underwent multiple lineup changes.

Originating in Enschede in 1967, the initial lineup comprised Hilda Felix (vocals), Henk Westendorp (vocals, later in Superfly),

John Snuverink (vocals, guitar), Frans Schaddelee (bass), Koos Versteeg (vocals & keys), and Rudi Nijhuis (drums).

By 1971, only Koos and Rudi remained, and new members like Getty Kaspers (vocals), John Gaasbeek (bass), Chris De Wolde (guitar), and Ard Weenink joined. Under CNR Records and producer Eddy Ouwens, they released their first single, "Spoke the Lord Creator," in 1972, followed by hits like "Fly Away," "In the Summernight," and "Tennessee Town" in 1974.

The band faced challenges in the disco era but adapted with a new look and sound. Hits like "Dear John" and a theme song for a Dutch TV charity show in 1978 and 1979 kept them in the charts. However, by 1980, their single "Regrets" marked the end as the group disbanded.

In 1997, the original lineup, including Getty Kaspers, re-recorded old hits and planned a tour. Getty pursued a solo career, and in 1979, she, along with John Gaasbeek and Wilma van Diepen, formed the Balloon Trio. Teach-In reunited in 2007 to perform "Ding-a-Dong" and again at the Eurovision Song Contest 2021 as an interval act.

Ding-a-dong (originally titled "Ding dinge dong" in Dutch, as indicated in the broadcast titles) was crafted by the musical talents of Dick Bakker, Will Luikinga, and Eddy Ouwens. This musical creation reached the pinnacle, securing the top position in both the Swiss and Norwegian Singles Charts.

Historically, "Ding-a-dong" stood out among Eurovision winners for its whimsical or entirely nonsensical titles or lyrics, echoing the spirit of Massiel's "La La La" in 1968 and Lulu's "Boom Bang-a-Bang" in 1969, and later followed by the Herreys' "Diggi-Loo Diggi-Ley" in 1984. The song was performed first on the night of the competition and marked the inception of the now-familiar

Eurovision voting system. Despite the tradition of favouring later performances, "Ding-a-dong" amassed 152 points, clinching the top spot in a field of nineteen. This win defied the norm that success usually favoured songs performed later in the broadcast.

Performed entirely in English, the up-tempo anthem celebrates positive thinking despite being written in a minor key. The lyrics encourage singing a song that goes "ding ding-a-dong" during moments of unhappiness, with the chorus asserting, "Ding-a-dong every hour when you pick a flower. Even when your lover is gone, gone, gone."

In the original Dutch version, "ding-a-dong" symbolises the singer's heartbeat recalling a past separation from a lover. Alongside "ding-a-dong," the lyrics feature "bim-bam-bom," representing a fearful heartbeat, and "tikke-(tikke)-tak" for the ticking of the clock while waiting for the lover's return. The song, reaching No.13 in the UK Singles Chart, also saw Teach-In record a German version. This catchy tune remains a memorable piece in the Eurovision Song Contest's rich history.

Leaderboard		
Year	Country	Victories
1957, 1959, 1969, 1975	**Netherlands**	**4**
1961, 1965, 1972, 1973	Luxembourg	4
1958, 1960, 1962, 1969	France	4
1968, 1969	Spain	2
1967, 1969	United Kingdom	2
1974	Sweden	1
1971	Monaco	1
1970	Ireland	1
1966	Austria	1
1963	Denmark	1

| Top Scores - 1975 |||||
Country	Artist	Song	Points	Position
Netherlands	Teach-In	"Ding-a-dong"	152	1
United Kingdom	The Shadows	"Let Me Be the One"	138	2
Italy	Wess and Dori Ghezzi	"Era"	115	3
France	Nicole	"Et bonjour à toi l'artiste"	91	4
Luxembourg	Géraldine	"Toi"	84	5

1976

The 1976 Eurovision Song Contest marked the 21st edition, hosted in **The Hague, Netherlands.** The European Broadcasting Union (EBU) and host broadcaster Nederlandse Omroep Stichting (NOS) orchestrated the competition, which unfolded at the Nederlands Congrescentrum on 3rd April 1976. Corry Brokken, the Dutch Eurovision winner from 1957, took on the role of the host.

Eighteen countries participated, with Sweden, Malta, and Turkey opting out after their involvement the previous year. Malta stayed absent until 1991, while Austria and Greece made a return after their last appearances in 1972 and 1974, respectively.

The **United Kingdom** clinched victory in the contest with the **Brotherhood of Man's** song "**Save Your Kisses for Me.**" This winning single went on to be the highest-selling in Eurovision history, securing a remarkable 80.39% of the maximum possible score and an average of 9.65 out of 12—a record under the voting system introduced in 1975.

The Hague serves as the governmental seat of the Kingdom of the Netherlands and the capital of the province of South Holland. As the third-largest city in the Netherlands, it stands behind Amsterdam and Rotterdam. Positioned in the west of the country, The Hague resides in the centre of the Haaglanden conurbation and occupies the southwest corner of the larger Randstad conurbation.

An interesting note on Sweden's absence: Sveriges Radio (SR), the broadcaster, refrained from participating due to financial constraints in hosting another contest if Sweden emerged victorious again. A new rule was consequently introduced, mandating each participating broadcaster to contribute to the staging costs. Additionally, public demonstrations against the contest in Sweden, as highlighted by author and historian John Kennedy O'Connor in his book "The Eurovision Song Contest – The Official History," played a role in SR's decision to abstain.

Brotherhood of Man, originating in 1969 under the guidance of Tony Hiller, emerged as a versatile British pop group with a dynamic lineup. The quartet, consisting of Martin Lee, Lee Sheriden, Nicky Stevens, and Sandra Stevens, solidified in 1973, bringing a distinctive harmony to their sound. Their achievements in the UK included three number-one singles and four top-twenty albums, with the group continuing to perform across Europe into the 21st century. Over their career, they produced 16 studio albums, boasting worldwide sales exceeding 15 million records.

Following their Eurovision triumph, the group sustained their popularity with hits like "Oh Boy (The Mood I'm In)" and "Figaro," showcasing their versatility in navigating changing musical landscapes. However, the late 1970s presented challenges, leading to a brief hiatus in the early 1980s.

The group's resilience became evident as they made a comeback with the 1982 single "Lightning Flash," signalling a new era in their musical journey. Their adaptability allowed them to stay relevant and resonate with audiences, setting their place in the charts once again.

Beyond their chart successes, Brotherhood of Man's impact on Eurovision is enduring, with their 1976 victory leaving an indelible mark on the contest's legacy. The group's ability to engage audiences with both timeless classics and contemporary hits showcases their enduring appeal.

The announcement of their retirement from touring in 2022 marked the end of an era, concluding a remarkable journey that spanned over four decades. Brotherhood of Man's legacy is not just in their chart-topping singles and Eurovision triumphs but also in their ability to evolve, adapt, and continue captivating audiences across generations. Their story remains a testament to the enduring power of harmonious melodies and timeless music.

Save Your Kisses for Me - The journey to Eurovision glory had its origins in Lee Sheriden's composition in August 1974. Initially named "Oceans of Love," the song faced a transformation into "Save Your Kisses for Me" after a year. Sheriden's persistence paid off, and the song became a pivotal part of the Brotherhood of Man's repertoire.

The Eurovision performance featured the group in distinctive black and white suits and red and white jumpsuits, delivering the song's narrative of a conflicted departure from a loved one in the morning, revealing a surprising twist in the final line—a three-year-old child. The performance earned the song an impressive 164 points, claiming victory with a significant margin over the second-placed entry.

"Not only did 'Save Your Kisses for Me' become the biggest-selling single for a winning Eurovision entry, but it also set a record for the highest relative score under the voting system introduced in 1975," averaging 9.65 points per jury. The song's success extended beyond Eurovision, reaching No.1 in various European countries and selling over six million copies globally. In the UK, it remained at No.1 for six weeks, achieving platinum certification and earning the title of the biggest-selling single of 1976.

Leaderboard		
Year	**Country**	**Victories**
1957, 1959, 1969, 1975	Netherlands	4
1961, 1965, 1972, 1973	Luxembourg	4
1958, 1960, 1962, 1969	France	4
1967, 1969, 1976	**United Kingdom**	**3**
1968, 1969	Spain	2
1974	Sweden	1
1971	Monaco	1
1970	Ireland	1
1966	Austria	1
1963	Denmark	1

Top Scores - 1976				
Country	**Artist**	**Song**	**Points**	**Position**
United Kingdom	Brotherhood of Man	"Save Your Kisses for Me"	164	1
France	Catherine Ferry	"Un, deux, trois"	147	2
Monaco	Mary Christy	"Toi, la musique et moi"	93	3
Switzerland	Peter, Sue and Marc	"Djambo Djambo"	91	4
Austria	Waterloo and Robinson	"My Little World"	80	5

1977

The 1977 Eurovision Song Contest marked the 22nd edition, hosted at the newly built Wembley Conference Centre in **London, United Kingdom**, on 7th May 1977. The competition, organised by the European Broadcasting Union (EBU) and hosted by the British Broadcasting Corporation (BBC), saw the return of Sweden and the absence of Yugoslavia.

Eighteen countries participated, while **France** emerged victorious with the song "**L'Oiseau et l'Enfant**," performed by **Marie Myriam**. The United Kingdom, Ireland, Monaco, and Greece secured the remaining top five positions, with Greece achieving its best result up to that point. France's win, their fifth in total, set a record at the time, holding strong for six years until Luxembourg matched it in 1983.

The chosen venue, Wembley Conference Centre, was the first purpose-built conference centre in the United Kingdom, inaugurated on 31st January 1977 and later demolished in 2006. The night of the contest drew an audience of 2,000 spectators.

In terms of participating countries, Tunisia withdrew after being drawn to perform fourth, and Yugoslavia chose not to participate until 1981. Sweden returned after a one-year absence. The language rule was reinstated, with Germany and Belgium permitted to sing in English due to having chosen their songs before the rule's reintroduction.

Originally scheduled for 2nd April 1977, the contest was postponed by a month due to a strike by BBC cameramen and technicians, making it the first Eurovision Song Contest held in May since its inception. The broadcast lacked postcards between songs due to strikes and time constraints, with the intended footage scrapped and replaced by shots of the audience.

Despite challenges, the contest proceeded, and final scores were adjusted after the live show due to errors in score announcements. Greece and France both duplicated scores, with subsequent deductions for certain countries, although these adjustments didn't alter the final song placements.

Marie Myriam, originally born as Myriam Lopes on 8th May 1957 in Luluabourg, Belgian Congo (now the Democratic Republic of the Congo), is a French singer of Portuguese descent.

In 1981, Myriam once again took the stage for France at the Yamaha Music Festival, delivering the song "Sentimentale" and securing the ninth position. In more recent times, she has been entrusted with announcing the votes of the French Jury at the Eurovision Song Contest.

Marie Myriam graced the 50th-anniversary concert in Copenhagen, Denmark, in October 2005, assuming the roles of a guest presenter and performer. During the same year, she penned the introduction for the French edition of "The Eurovision Song Contest – The Official History" by John Kennedy O'Connor.

Myriam shared her life with music producer Michel Elmosnino from the late 1970s until his passing at the age of 67 on 20th December 2013.

L'Oiseau et l'Enfant - ("The Bird and the Child") was crafted by Jean-Paul Cara and penned by Joe Gracy; this composition currently holds the distinction of being the last French song to secure victory in the contest.

Taking the stage as the eighteenth and final performance of the night, following Belgium's Dream Express with "A Million in One, Two, Three," the song amassed a remarkable 136 points, claiming the top spot among eighteen competitors. Myriam showcased her versatility by recording the song in five languages: French, English (as "The Bird and the Child"), German ("Der Vogel und das Mädchen"), Spanish ("El zagal y el ave azul"), and her mother tongue, Portuguese ("A ave e a infância").

During Preview Week, Myriam's music video depicted her enchanting performance in the open-air setting of Square René Viviani in Paris. Notably, the preview video featured gendarmes restraining the enthusiastic crowd, some of whom had scaled the renowned "oldest tree in Paris" for a glimpse of the singer. On the night of the contest, Myriam graced the stage in an elegant floor-length orange gown while her five backup singers donned black attire.

In 2016, the UNICEF project Kids United paid tribute to the timeless piece, covering it in their second album, "Tout le bonheur du monde." The rendition made its mark on the SNEP singles charts in August 2016. Furthermore, a cover of the song found its place in a 2021 IKEA advertisement in Canada.

Leaderboard		
Year	Country	Victories
1958, 1960, 1962, 1969, 1977	**France**	**5**
1957, 1959, 1969, 1975	Netherlands	4
1961, 1965, 1972, 1973	Luxembourg	4
1967, 1969, 1976	United Kingdom	3
1968, 1969	Spain	2
1974	Sweden	1
1971	Monaco	1

1970	Ireland	1
1966	Austria	1
1963	Denmark	1

Top Scores - 1977

Country	Artist	Song	Points	Position
France	Marie Myriam	"L'Oiseau et l'Enfant"	136	1
United Kingdom	Lynsey de Paul & Mike Moran	"Rock Bottom"	121	2
Ireland	The Swarbriggs Plus Two	"It's Nice to Be in Love Again"	119	3
Monaco	Michèle Torr	"Une petite française"	96	4
Greece	Pascalis, Marianna, Robert & Bessy	"Mathema solfege"	92	5

1978

The 1978 Contest marked the 23rd edition, hosted in **Paris, France**. The European Broadcasting Union (EBU) and host broadcaster Télévision Française 1 (TF1) organised the contest at the Palais des Congrès on 22nd April 1978.

Presented by French television hosts Denise Fabre and Léon Zitrone, this edition was notable for having more than one presenter for the first time since 1956 and featuring a male presenter. **Twenty countries** participated, marking the highest number in the competition's history at that time.

Israel emerged as the winner with the song "**A-Ba-Ni-Bi**" performed by **Izhar Cohen & the Alphabeta**. The winning entry, a love song sung in Hebrew, marked Israel's first Eurovision victory and the first winning song performed in a Semitic language. Nurit Hirsh conducted the winning song, making her the first woman to do so. Unfortunately, Norway finished last, receiving the first nul points after the new voting system was implemented in 1975.

Denmark returned to the competition after a twelve-year absence, and Turkey made a comeback after missing the previous two years.

Izhar Cohen, born on 13th March 13th 1951, is a Tel Aviv native raised in Givatayim from a family of Yemenite-Jewish descent. From childhood, Cohen immersed himself in singing, often joining his father in performances. At 18, he became part of the IDF's Nachal entertainment troupe. In the 1970s, Cohen became one of Israel's most-played singers.

Cohen later represented Israel again in 1985 with an unnamed group, performing "Olé, Olé" and finishing 5th. Despite attempts in 1982, 1987, and 1996, he didn't secure victory in the national finals.

An actor in the Haifa Theatre, Cohen also owns a jewellery shop on Dizengoff Street in Tel Aviv. He participated in "The Singer in the Mask" as "Bull," achieving 10th place overall.

Alphabeta, the group accompanying Cohen, comprised Reuven Erez, Lisa Gold-Rubin, Nehama Shutan, Esther Tzuberi, and Itzhak Okev. Their winning song, "A-Ba-Ni-Bi," earned Israel five consecutive maximum 12 points, setting a Eurovision Song Contest record with a total score of 157 points. As Israel's victory became apparent, Jordan abruptly halted its live broadcast, citing technical difficulties, and replaced it with an image of daffodils. A day later, Jordan presented the Belgian song, which came second as the winner. Despite the initial motivation for sending Cohen's song due to perceived inadequacies in the national competition, he remained confident of his victory.

A-Ba-Ni-Bi, written in Hebrew as א-ב-ני-בי and inspired by the bet-language game for the word אני (aní), meaning "I" in Hebrew.

The song, a collaboration between lyricist Ehud Manor and composer-conductor Nurit Hirsh, pioneers an up-tempo disco style, foreshadowing later performances in the competition. Despite initial criticism of its title, "A-Ba-Ni-Bi" is regarded by many fans as one of the better entries in Eurovision history.

The lyrics explore childhood perceptions of love, contrasting secret childhood affections with the idea that adulthood should embrace love openly. The Bet language, a children's language game, is incorporated, playfully transforming the phrase "I love you" into "A-Ba-Ni-Bi." Despite some confusion in its title presentation, the song's musical uniqueness lies in its abrupt ending after the key change, deviating from the typical structure of Eurovision entries.

During the contest, Cohen and the backing vocalists (Reuven Erez, Itzhak Okev, Lisa Gold-Rubin, Nehama Shutan, and Esther Tzuberi) wore white clothing and delivered a mostly stationary performance, swaying in time to the music. The song, performed eighteenth on the night, garnered 157 points, placing first in a field of 20 and receiving points from every voting country except Sweden.

The song found new life in a parody by Turkish group Grup Vitamin and was performed by Israeli singer Netta Barzilai on a one-stringed guitar in 2018, the year she won the Eurovision Song Contest.

Leaderboard		
Year	Country	Victories
1958, 1960, 1962, 1969, 1977	France	5
1957, 1959, 1969, 1975	Netherlands	4
1961, 1965, 1972, 1973	Luxembourg	4
1967, 1969, 1976	United Kingdom	3
1968, 1969	Spain	2
1978	**Israel**	**1**
1974	Sweden	1
1971	Monaco	1
1970	Ireland	1
1966	Austria	1

Top Scores - 1978			
Country	Artist	Song	Points	Position
Israel	Izhar Cohen & the Alphabeta	"A-Ba-Ni-Bi"	157	1
Belgium	Jean Vallée	"L'Amour ça fait chanter la vie"	125	2

France	Joël Prévost	"Il y aura toujours des violons"	119	3
Monaco	Caline & Olivier Toussaint	"Les Jardins de Monaco"	107	4
Ireland	Colm C. T. Wilkinson	"Born to Sing"	86	5

1979

The 24th edition took place at the International Convention Centre on 31st March 1979 in **Jerusalem, Israel**. Organised by the European Broadcasting Union (EBU) and hosted by the Israeli Broadcasting Authority (IBA). The competition was hosted by Israeli television presenter Daniel Pe'er and singer Yardena Arazi, making it the first time the Eurovision Song Contest ventured outside Europe.

Nineteen countries participated in the contest, with Turkey opting out due to pressure from Arab countries against participating in an event hosted by Israel. Yugoslavia also abstained from the competition for political reasons, despite a substantial public desire for their return, as evidenced by a poll in which almost 100,000 people expressed the wish for Yugoslavia to rejoin. For the second consecutive year, **Israel** clinched victory with the song "**Hallelujah**," performed by the Israeli group **Milk and Honey (featuring Gali Atari)**

The emblem of the contest creatively merged a G-clef, the IBA logo, and the names of all participating countries, arranged in the order of their appearance. Dov Ben David conceived the stage design, incorporating a dynamic symbol inspired by the IBA logo, resembling a lamp with three concentric rings. The symbol was animated using a small projected model.

As Israeli Television had not yet embraced colour broadcasting (except for select occasions), cameras were borrowed from the BBC—a situation reminiscent of when RTÉ hosted the 1971 contest in Dublin. Under the direction of conductor Izhak Graziani, the IBA Symphony Orchestra provided musical accompaniment for each song, except the Italian entry, which opted not to use the orchestra. Notably, this contest featured an orchestra composed of 39 musicians, a unique occurrence.

In a departure from the norm, the interludes between songs showcased mime artists instead of the participating singers. The Yoram Boker Mime Group, featuring prominent Israeli mime artists like Ezra Dagan and Hanoch Rozen, performed against a backdrop of illustrations by Dudu Geva and Yochanan Lakitzevitz, showcasing landmarks and landscapes of the respective countries.

The contest overview revealed a post-broadcast adjustment to the scores due to a misunderstanding by presenter Yardena Arazi during the voting announcement. Spain initially appeared to award 10 points to both Portugal and Israel, but post-programme verification corrected this, reducing Portugal's score by four points to 64. The intermission featured the Shalom '79 Dancing Ensemble, presenting a lively performance of Israeli Folk Dances in a medley directed by the ensemble's manager and choreographer, Gavri Levy.

Milk and Honey, known in Hebrew as חלב ודבש (Khalav U'Dvash), was an Israeli vocal ensemble initially comprised of Shmulik Bilu, Reuven Gvirtz, Yehuda Tamir, and **Gali Atari**.

Formed in 1978 by producer Shlomo Zach and composer Kobi Oshrat, Milk and Honey emerged as an ensemble after both Hakol Over Habibi and Yardena Arazi declined the opportunity to perform Oshrat's song "Hallelujah" in the Israeli national selection for the Eurovision Song Contest 1979.

Within a year after the song contest, Gali Atari retired from Milk and Honey, and Leah Lupatin replaced her in 1981. Atari later filed a lawsuit against Zach for unpaid royalties. In 1994, an Israeli court ruled in Atari's favour, ordering Zach to settle the unpaid royalties. In 2003, Zach and his partners filed a lawsuit against Oshrat, contending that Oshrat should have contributed to the payments made to Atari as a group partner. This legal dispute reached a resolution through mediation in 2009.

Milk and Honey continued their participation in the national final on two subsequent occasions. In 1981, they performed "Serenada," securing a fourth-place finish. In 1989, with "Ani Ma'amin," they attained an eighth-place position. Additionally, Gvirtz and Tamir supported the Israeli Song Contest Act in 1988

Hallelujah, originally submitted by composer Kobi Oshrat for the national Israeli selection in 1978, faced rejection for being deemed insufficiently strong. It also faced rejection at song festivals in Chile and Japan. However, the song found its moment in the national selection for the 1979 Eurovision contest. Initially intended for the band Hakol Over Habibi, the opportunity was declined, leading to the formation of the group Milk and Honey. The song narrowly won the national selection with 63 points, just two more than the runner-up.

This marked the fourth instance of the host country winning the Eurovision contest, a feat previously achieved by Switzerland, Spain, and Luxembourg. Due to the scheduling clash with Yom Hazikaron, Israel's Memorial Day, the country couldn't host or participate in the next contest. The unique performance of "Hallelujah," with Atari and her backing singers entering the stage individually, contributed to its recognition as a classic of the contest and a modern Jewish standard.

Performed tenth on the night, "Hallelujah" secured 125 points, placing 1st in a field of 19. Notably, it was the first time the winning song had come from behind to clinch victory on the final vote, with the Spanish jury's vote tipping the scales.

"Hallelujah" experienced reprisals at later Eurovision events, including a tribute in 1999 for the Balkan wars' victims, a performance by Gali Atari during the 'Switch Song' interval act in the Eurovision Song Contest 2019, and a sing-along during Eurovision: Europe Shine a Light in 2020. To commemorate Israel's 70th year of independence, an updated version was released featuring Gali Atari and pop superstar Eden Ben Zaken. In 2019, Atari refused to sing with her former teammates and instead performed with other Eurovision participants, including Conchita Wurst, Måns Zelmerlöw, Eleni Foureira, and Verka Serduchka.

Leaderboard		
Year	Country	Victories
1958, 1960, 1962, 1969, 1977	France	5
1957, 1959, 1969, 1975	Netherlands	4
1961, 1965, 1972, 1973	Luxembourg	4
1967, 1969, 1976	United Kingdom	3
1978, 1979	**Israel**	**2**
1968, 1969	Spain	2
1974	Sweden	1
1971	Monaco	1
1970	Ireland	1
1966	Austria	1

Top Scores - 1979				
Country	Artist	Song	Points	Position
Israel	Milk & Honey	"Hallelujah"	125	1
Spain	Betty Missiego	"Su canción"	116	2
France	Anne-Marie David	"Je suis l'enfant soleil"	106	3
Germany	Dschinghis Khan	"Dschinghis Khan"	86	4
Ireland	Cathal Dunne	"Happy Man"	80	5

1980

The 25th edition of the competition unfolded in **The Hague, Netherlands**, orchestrated by host broadcaster Nederlandse Omroep Stichting (NOS) and the European Broadcasting Union (EBU). Originally, Israel, the winner of the 1979 contest, declined to host due to the scheduling clash with the Yom HaZikaron holiday, marking the first instance of the previous year's winner not competing.

Despite Spain and the United Kingdom also turning down the opportunity, the Netherlands stepped in, agreeing to host the show on the 19th of April, 1980.

Nineteen countries took part, and Morocco joined the contest, making its only appearance. Monaco also opted out and did not return until 2004. The winner was **Johnny Logan**, representing **Ireland** with the song "**What's Another Year**".

Dutch actress Marlous Fluitsma took on the role of host, though individual presenters from participating nations introduced each song. The scoring system, introduced in 1975, remained consistent, with each country's jury assigning 12, 10, 8, 7, 6, 5, 4, 3, 2, 1 point(s) to their top ten songs. However, in a new twist, countries were obliged to announce their scores in ascending order—1, 2, 3, and so on. This change added an element of anticipation as viewers waited for each country to reveal their highest 12 points at the conclusion of each voting round.

During the voting sequence, Marlous Fluitsma utilised a distinctive telephone to communicate with the nineteen jury spokespersons. It is worth noting that the phones were merely props and not functional connections.

Johnny Logan is the professional name for Seán Patrick Michael Sherrard, an Irish singer and musician renowned for being the first artist to secure victory as a lead singer at the Eurovision Song Contest on two occasions.

Logan achieved his first Eurovision win in 1980 with the chart-topping song "What's Another Year," triumphing in eight countries. His second victory came in 1987 with "Hold Me Now," reaching No.1 in Israel, Ireland, and Belgium and ranking within the top ten in ten other music markets. For 36 years, he stood as the sole artist with two Eurovision victories until Loreen's second win in 2023.

Apart from his singing career, Logan has also composed two Eurovision songs for Linda Martin, contributing "Terminal 3" in 1984 (second place) and "Why Me?" in 1992 (first place). This accomplishment places Logan among the select few who have composed two winning Eurovision entries.

Born on the 13th of May 1954 in Frankston, Victoria, Australia, Logan hails from a musical background, with his father, Charles Alphonsus Sherrard, known as Patrick O'Hagan, being a Derry-born Irish tenor. The family relocated to Ireland when Logan was three, and he displayed an early interest in music, learning the guitar and composing songs by the age of 13. Logan's initial claim to fame came with his roles in Irish musicals like "Adam and Eve" (1977) and "Joseph and the Amazing Technicolor Dreamcoat" (Joseph).

Often dubbed "Mister Eurovision," Logan remains an active performer and songwriter. His success includes platinum-selling albums in Scandinavia, such as "The Irish Connection" (2007). He has also ventured into musical theatre, participating in productions like "Excalibur."

In popular culture, Logan has appeared on TV shows like "Never Mind the Buzzcocks" (2002) and featured in advertisements. He received attention for comments on Jedward, the Irish Eurovision entry in 2011, clarifying that he found them embarrassing to watch.

Logan is known for rarely giving media interviews, citing frequent misquotations.

What's Another Year was crafted by Shay Healy and originally intended for showband frontman Glen Curtin, who declined the opportunity; the song underwent rearrangement by Bill Whelan to suit Johnny Logan's distinctive singing style. Notably, Whelan later composed "Riverdance" for the 1994 Eurovision Song Contest. The song's recognisable saxophone introduction, performed by Scottish musician Colin Tully, adds a distinctive musical touch.

"What's Another Year" proved pivotal in Logan's Eurovision success, foreshadowing triumphs in 1987 with "Hold Me Now" and a win as the songwriter for Linda Martin's "Why Me?" in 1992. The track's enduring popularity was acknowledged when it was selected as one of the 14 greatest Eurovision entries in a special commemoration of the contest's 50th anniversary. Shane MacGowan of The Pogues covered the song for the Eurotrash cover album in 1998.

Famously, upon winning the Contest, Logan, overwhelmed with emotion, couldn't reach the high notes in the song's reprise. Instead, he passionately exclaimed, "I love you, Ireland," a sentiment he would echo seven years later.

Performing seventeenth on the night, the song garnered 143 points at the close of voting, securing the top spot among a field of 19.

Johnny Logan's enduring connection with the song is evident in his releases of German and Spanish-language versions. During the Eurovision: Europe Shine a Light special in 2020, Logan delivered a live performance of the song from a studio in Dublin, backed by the show's presenters and a chorus of Eurovision Song Contest fans worldwide. A video showcasing Logan's three Eurovision wins was featured during the instrumental bridge of the performance.

Leaderboard		
Year	Country	Victories
1958, 1960, 1962, 1969, 1977	France	5
1957, 1959, 1969, 1975	Netherlands	4
1961, 1965, 1972, 1973	Luxembourg	4
1967, 1969, 1976	United Kingdom	3
1970, 1980	**Ireland**	**2**
1978, 1979	Israel	2
1968, 1969	Spain	2
1974	Sweden	1
1971	Monaco	1
1966	Austria	1

Top Scores - 1980				
Country	Artist	Song	Points	Position
Ireland	Johnny Logan	"What's Another Year"	143	1
Germany	Katja Ebstein	"Theater"	128	2
United Kingdom	Prima Donna	"Love Enough for Two"	106	3
Switzerland	Paola	"Cinéma"	104	4
Netherlands	Maggie MacNeal	"Amsterdam"	93	5

1981

The 1981 Contest marked the 26th edition, held in **Dublin, Ireland**. The venue for this musical spectacle was the RDS Simmonscourt, where on 4th April 1981, Irish television journalist Doireann Ní Bhriain guided the audience through the festivities.

A total of **twenty countries** participated, matching the record set in the 1978 edition. Cyprus made its debut, and after brief absences, Israel and Yugoslavia returned to the competition. Notably, Morocco and Italy opted out of participating.

The **United Kingdom** secured victory with the song "**Making Your Mind Up**," performed by **Bucks Fizz**; Germany claimed the second position for the second consecutive year, while France secured the third spot. Norway found itself at the bottom yet again, with its third instance of scoring zero points in the contest.

The participant lineup underwent changes as Monaco withdrew its interest, reducing the initial count to 21 countries. Cyprus made its debut and finished in sixth place. Israel returned after a one-year hiatus, securing the seventh position. Yugoslavia also re-entered the competition after a five-year absence. Italy chose not to participate due to a lack of interest. Also, Morocco declined to participate despite debuting the previous year. The reasons behind Morocco's withdrawal were not explicitly stated, but speculation points to their unsatisfactory placement in the 1980 contest and geopolitical considerations involving other Arab nations avoiding engagement with Israel. The draw for the running order took place on 14th November 1980, confirming a total of 20 entrants.

Bucks Fizz was a British pop group formed in 1981; the group was comprised of four vocalists: Bobby G, Cheryl Baker, Mike Nolan, and Jay Aston. They gained popularity for their unique dance routine, where the male members of the group would rip off the female members' skirts to reveal mini-skirts. They had a successful career, especially in the UK, where they had three No.1 singles and were one of the best-selling groups of the 80s. They have sold over 50 million records globally. Over the years, the group's line-up has changed.

After a sold-out gig in Newcastle, the Bucks Fizz tour bus collided with an articulated lorry on 11 December 1984. Although no one died, several crew members, including all the members of Bucks Fizz, suffered injuries. Mike Nolan had the worst injuries and fell into a coma for three days. He awoke from the coma but suffered from epilepsy, short-term memory loss, and vision loss. Bobby G was treated for whiplash, Jay Aston was hospitalised for back and head injuries, and Cheryl Baker broke three vertebrae in her spine. The members helped set up the HeadFirst charity for crash victims. The original line-up (Nolan, Baker, and Aston) played a benefit concert for the charity in 2009.

In 1985, tensions mounted within the group and Jay Aston quit; after this, the group hired Shelley Preston and signed a new contract with Polydor. They released successful singles, including "New Beginning (Mamba Seyra)" and "Heart of Stone," but eventually disbanded as a recording group. The group continued as a live act with a changing line-up, with Baker eventually leaving to pursue a career in television and the rest of the group adding new members. In 1997, Bobby G. and David Van Day had a dispute, leading to Van Day forming a new version of the group with Mike Nolan. However, both versions of the group failed to succeed and faced criticism from fans. By 2001, Nolan left Van Day's group, and Van Day continued touring with new members.

Making Your Mind Up was composed by Andy Hill and John Danter and released in March 1981 as the group's debut single, only two months after they were formed. The song was a success, reaching No.1 in the UK and several other countries, with over four million copies sold. It was included in the group's self-titled debut album and launched their career, leading to their status as one of the biggest-selling acts of the 1980s.

The song was recorded at Mayfair Studios in London with RCA Records, with backing vocals supplied by Alan Carvell. The song was co-published by Paper Music, owned by Billy Lawrie, a songwriter and brother of singer Lulu. Choreographer Chrissie Whickham worked with the group on the dance routine. The lyrics of the song can be interpreted as making the decision to commit to a serious relationship.

Leaderboard		
Year	Country	Victories
1958, 1960, 1962, 1969, 1977	France	5
1967, 1969, 1976, 1981	**United Kingdom**	**4**
1957, 1959, 1969, 1975	Netherlands	4
1961, 1965, 1972, 1973	Luxembourg	4
1970, 1980	Ireland	2
1978, 1979	Israel	2
1968, 1969	Spain	2
1974	Sweden	1
1971	Monaco	1
1966	Austria	1

Top Scores - 1981				
Country	Artist	Song	Points	Position
United Kingdom	Bucks Fizz	"Making Your Mind Up"	136	1
Germany	Lena Valaitis	"Johnny Blue"	132	2

France	Jean Gabilou	"Humanahum"	125	3
Switzerland	Peter, Sue & Marc	"Io senza te"	121	4
Ireland	Sheeba	"Horoscopes"	105	5

1982

The 27th edition of The Eurovision Song Contest unfolded at the Harrogate International Centre in the **United Kingdom** on 24th April 1982, under the guidance of English TV presenter Jan Leeming.

A total of **eighteen countries** participated, with Greece opting out for the year and France withdrawing due to the downsizing of their national broadcasters. **Germany** secured victory with the song "**Ein bißchen Frieden**" by **Nicole**, marking their first win after participating consistently since the contest's inception.

Harrogate, situated in North Yorkshire, England, known historically as 'The English Spa,' became the host venue for the contest. The town's roots date back to the 17th century when it amalgamated two smaller settlements, High Harrogate and Low Harrogate. Renowned for its spa waters and RHS Harlow Carr gardens, Harrogate attracted visitors seeking the health benefits of its 'chalybeate' waters in the 17th and 18th centuries.

Notably, 1982 saw a record low of 18 participating countries, a figure unmatched in subsequent editions. Greece had initially planned to participate but withdrew their entry, "Sarantapente kopelies" by Themis Adamantidis, due to concerns about its quality. In a similar vein, France's TF1 declined participation, with Pierre Bouteiller, the head of entertainment, criticising the lack of talent and mediocre songs. Antenne 2 took over as the new broadcaster, ensuring France's return to the contest in 1983.

Nicole Seibert, formerly known as Nicole, is a distinguished German singer, songwriter, musician, and producer born on 25th October 1964 in Saarbrücken, Saarland, West Germany. With a prolific career, Nicole has released over 25 studio albums and 80 singles, showcasing her versatility in languages like English, Dutch, and French. She has also contributed as a songwriter for some of her compositions.

In her early years, Nicole commenced her musical journey at the age of four and achieved commercial success at 16 with her debut single, "Flieg nicht so hoch, mein kleiner Freund," reaching No.2 in Austria and securing Top 40 positions across European charts.

Throughout her career, Nicole continued to release albums, with notable ones in 1982 titled "Ein bißchen Frieden" (German) and "A Little Peace" (English). In 2005, she co-produced the album "Alles Fliesst," followed by "Mitten ins Herz" in 2008, accompanied by an "unplugged" tour.

Nicole's musical journey evolved as she collaborated with renowned composers such as Ralph Siegel, Bernd Meinunger, Robert Jung, and Jean Frankfurter in her early years. In 2016, she collaborated with Siegel and Meinunger on the studio album "Traumfänger" and continued to explore diverse partnerships in subsequent works.

Her personal life reveals her roots in Nohfelden, Saarland, where she grew up in a family of four children. She married Winfried Seibert, her childhood friend, in 1984, and they have two children. Known for her spiritual beliefs and concerts in churches, Nicole remains committed to humanitarian causes, advocating for child abuse prevention, homeless children's well-being, and supporting campaigns against Rett syndrome and "life without chains." Her resilience and success have left an indelible mark on the music industry for over four decades.

Ein bißchen Frieden (translated as "A Bit of Peace") stands as a German-language song crafted by the prolific German Eurovision-writing duo Ralph Siegel (music) and Bernd Meinunger (lyrics).

Following her triumph at The Eurovision Song Contest, Nicole delivered a reprise of "Ein bißchen Frieden" in four languages: German, English, French, and Dutch. This spontaneous decision, made on the spur of the moment, surprised her backing group. Expanding the song's reach, Nicole released recordings in five additional languages across Europe: Danish, Italian, Russian, and combinations of German-English-Dutch and German-English-Italian. The song ascended to the top of the charts in numerous countries, and the English version achieved the distinction of being the last Eurovision winner to claim the number-one spot in the United Kingdom. Furthermore, the English version holds the historic significance of becoming the 500th British Number One.

The English rendition, titled "A Little Peace" and translated by Paul Greedus, was released in predominantly English-speaking territories, securing the top position on the charts in the UK and Ireland, among others. According to composer and producer Ralph Siegel, the single achieved impressive sales figures, ranging from 2.5 to 3 million copies.

The song earned further accolades when it was selected in a 2005 internet poll by the European Broadcasting Union as one of the 14 most popular songs in Eurovision history. It also featured in the Congratulations 50th-anniversary concert in Copenhagen, Denmark, in October 2005, where it finished as the seventh most popular song in the history of the contest.

The enduring appeal of "A Little Peace" led to various cover versions. Daniel O'Donnell covered the English version for his 1997 album, "I Believe."

In different languages, "Ein bißchen Frieden" found new life as "Malo miru" in Slovene by Irena Tratnik and Oto Pestner, "Jsme děti slunce" in Czech by Jaromír Mayer, "Malo mira" in Croatian by Ana Štefok, "En smule fred" in Danish by Susanne Lana, "Egy kis nyugalmat kívánok én" in Hungarian by Neoton Família, "Troszeczkę ziemi, troszeczkę słońca" in Polish by Eleni Tzoka, "Un poco de paz" in Spanish by Mexican singer Laura Flores, and "Vain Hieman Rauhaa" in Finnish by Katri Helena. Notably, the Swedish band Rednex covered "Ein bißchen Frieden" in 1996.

Additionally, German techno-punk band DAF released "Ein bißchen Krieg" ("A Bit of War") as a response to the perceived sentimentality of the original song. German comedy metal band J.B.O. contributed a parody cover in Rammstein style in 1997 on their album "Laut!"

Leaderboard		
Year	Country	Victories
1958, 1960, 1962, 1969, 1977	France	5
1967, 1969, 1976, 1981	United Kingdom	4
1957, 1959, 1969, 1975	Netherlands	4
1961, 1965, 1972, 1973	Luxembourg	4
1970, 1980	Ireland	2
1978, 1979	Israel	2
1968, 1969	Spain	2
1982	**Germany**	**1**
1974	Sweden	1
1971	Monaco	1
1966	Austria	1

Top Scores - 1982				
Country	Artist	Song	Points	Position
Germany	Nicole	"Ein bißchen Frieden"	161	1
Israel	Avi Toledano	"Hora"	100	2
Switzerland	Arlette Zola	"Amour on t'aime"	97	3
Belgium	Stella	"Si tu aimes ma musique"	96	4
Cyprus	Anna Vissi	"Mono i agapi"	85	5

1983

The 1983 Eurovision Song Contest marked the 28th instalment, hosted in **Munich, West Germany**. Despite it being Germany's inaugural victory, the country had previously hosted the competition in 1957. The European Broadcasting Union (EBU), along with host broadcasters Arbeitsgemeinschaft der öffentlich-rechtlichen Rundfunkanstalten der Bundesrepublik Deutschland (ARD) and Bayerischer Rundfunk (BR), organised the event at the Rudi-Sedlmayer-Halle on 23rd of April 1983, with the hosting duties undertaken by German dancer Marlene Charell.

This edition featured **twenty participating countries**, including the return of France, Greece, and Italy, while Ireland opted not to participate. **Luxembourg** emerged victorious with **Corinne Hermès**' "**Si la vie est cadeau**," equalling France's record of five victories set in 1977. Notably, the winning entry was performed last for the second consecutive year, and Israel secured second place for the second year running. Unfortunately, Spain and Turkey ended up with no points, continuing the trend of at least one country receiving nul points for the third consecutive year.

The 1983 contest made history by being the first to be televised in Australia, marking the beginning of its popularity in the country, eventually leading to Australia's debut in the contest in 2015.

Munich, the capital of the Bavarian state, hosted the event at the Rudi-Sedlmayer-Halle. The venue, initially named after the president of the Bavarian State Sport Association, opened in 1972 for the basketball events of the Summer Olympics. Due to production needs, the arena's 5500 seats were reduced to 3200 for the final night, with 2000 reserved for delegations and journalists and 1200 available for the general public.

Preparations for the production began in June 1982, with Bayerischer Rundfunk as the main producer, incurring costs of 1.2 million DM. Through donations and contributions, the broadcaster managed to reduce expenses to about 1 million DM. Munich contributed 60,000 DM for a reception for participating delegations.

Various receptions and events took place in the lead-up to the final. The presentation format saw the introduction of countries without pre-filmed "postcards." Marlene Charell, the hostess, made announcements in German, followed by translations in French and English. Language issues during the voting and introductions extended the contest past three hours.

Corinne Hermès, born Corinne Bondeaux on the 16th of November 1961, is a renowned French singer. Corinne's musical journey commenced in 1974, marked by her victory in a singing contest in Roquebrune-sur-Argens. Five years later, during the recording of her single "La ville où je vis / Le blouson gris," composer and producer Bernard Estardy discovered her exceptional voice. Estardy offered her the leading female role in his musical comedy, "36 Front Populaire," a project that unfortunately never came to fruition due to political considerations.

In 1983, Corinne was internally selected by RTL to represent Luxembourg in the 28th Eurovision Song Contest. Her captivating performance of "Si la vie est cadeau," composed by Jean-Pierre Millers with lyrics by Alain Garcia, earned her 142 points, securing Luxembourg's fifth victory. This success, however, came with a slim margin of only 6 points over the runner-up, Israel's Ofra Haza.

Following her Eurovision victory, Corinne announced a new album, but only two songs, "Vivre à deux" and "Michaël," were released. In subsequent years, she released singles such as "Ma liberté" in 1986 and regained success in 1989 with "Dessine-moi," which reached the top 20 in France and peaked at No.2 in the Francophone Belgian charts. In 1990, she received recognition as the Best Female Révélation (Newcomer) at the Victoires de la Musique, causing controversy due to the song being published ten years prior.

Corinne's musical journey continued with notable contributions, including recording the theme tune "L'amour est artiste" for the TF1 drama "Les Grandes Marées" in 1993. She also participated in Eurovision-related events, representing France in the international jury for the Eurovision Song Contest 2000 and presenting the French vote points in 2001.

In 2006, she released a new album, "Vraie," featuring singles like "S'il n'y avait pas les mots" and "On vit comme on aime." Her extensive career is reflected in her compilations, including a best-of released in 2012. Corinne's 2019 album, "Intemporelle," showcases her timeless talent through covers of famous French and international songs.

Si la vie est cadeau ("If Life Is a Gift") - The song unfolds as a poignant ballad, exploring the profound marvel of life, drawing parallels between existence and a precious gift. Its lyrics depict the singer's emotional journey in love, where promises made by a man who pledged to the world were left unfulfilled. Expressing the pain of unmet expectations, the singer questions the fate of the child she envisioned giving birth to in the spring. Despite the heartache, she extends a poignant perspective on gifts, declaring their worth regardless of how they are bestowed – given, taken, or returned. The song subtly urges listeners to cherish fleeting moments, highlighting the brevity of joy.

Corinne Hermès lent her captivating vocals to alternate renditions of the song in English, titled "Words of Love," and in German, titled "Liebe gibt und nimmt" ("Love gives and takes").

Performed as the 20th entry on the Eurovision stage, it secured a remarkable victory with 142 points, claiming the top spot among 20 contestants. This triumph drew Luxembourg level with France, each boasting five contest victories. However, both nations would later be surpassed by Ireland and Sweden, each accumulating seven victories.

Despite its Eurovision success, "Si la vie est cadeau" achieved only moderate commercial acclaim compared to previous Eurovision winners. It reached notable chart positions, peaking at No.2 in France, No.3 in Belgium, No.12 in Ireland, No.13 in Sweden, No.14 in Switzerland, and No.19 in the Netherlands. The song, unfortunately, failed to make an impact on most other European charts.

The Finnish version, "Lahjan sain," was artistically rendered by Lea Laven, serving as the title track for her 1983 album release.

Leaderboard		
Year	Country	Victories
1961, 1965, 1972, 1973, 1983	**Luxembourg**	**5**
1958, 1960, 1962, 1969, 1977	France	5
1967, 1969, 1976, 1981	United Kingdom	4
1957, 1959, 1969, 1975	Netherlands	4
1970, 1980	Ireland	2
1978, 1979	Israel	2

1968, 1969	Spain	2
1982	Germany	1
1974	Sweden	1
1971	Monaco	1

Top Scores - 1983

Country	Artist	Song	Points	Position
Luxembourg	Corinne Hermès	"Si la vie est cadeau"	142	1
Israel	Ofra Haza	"Hi"	136	2
Sweden	Carola Häggkvist	"Främling"	126	3
Yugoslavia	Daniel	"Džuli"	125	4
Germany	Hoffmann & Hoffmann	"Rücksicht"	94	5

1984

Luxembourg City, Luxembourg held the 1984 Eurovision Song Contest, organised by The European Broadcasting Union (EBU) and host broadcaster Radio Télévision Luxembourg (RTL). The event took place at the Théâtre Municipal on the 5th of May 1984.

Nineteen countries participated in the contest, with Israel and Greece abstaining, while Ireland returned after sitting out the previous year. **Sweden** emerged victorious with the song "**Diggi-Loo Diggi-Ley**" by **Herreys**, marking the first Swedish-winning entry in their native language. Richard and Louis Herrey, aged 19 years and 260 days and 18 years and 184 days respectively, became the youngest adult Eurovision male winners.

Renowned stage designer Roland de Groot, known for his work in previous Eurovision contests, returned with a concept involving translucent panels suspended above the stage, creating unique backdrops for each performance. The live orchestra, positioned under the stage in a traditional orchestra pit, remained out of view on camera.

Désirée Nosbusch, a Luxembourg native residing in the USA, presented the show in an unconventional and relaxed manner. Speaking in English, French, German, and Luxembourgish interchangeably, she brought a distinctive hosting style to the competition.

In 1984, the postcards between songs featured "The Tourists," mime artists virtually exploring participant nations' tourist attractions using a combination of animated and real props, employing the Chroma key process.

The year 1984 is also remembered for audible booing from the audience, notably at the end of the UK's performance. Speculations suggest the booing may have stemmed from English football hooligans rioting in Luxembourg in November 1983 after failing to qualify for the 1984 UEFA European Football Championship.

As the penultimate jury's votes were tallied, a mere six-point difference separated Sweden and Ireland, with 141 and 135 points, respectively. Despite Portugal's two points from the last jury, they did not grant any points to Ireland, sealing their fate. Portugal's voting also affected Denmark, who briefly led the scoreboard but fell to third place when Portugal's 12 points boosted Spain. Despite the challenges, this marked Denmark's best position in over two decades.

Herreys, sometimes spelt Herrey's or Herrey, stands as a Swedish pop sensation comprised of three brothers: Per Herrey (born 9 August 1958), Richard Herrey (born 19 August 1964), and Louis Herrey (born 3 November 1966).

In 1985, the trio added another feather to their cap by winning the Sopot International Song Festival with the infectious track "Sommarparty." Notably, during their Eurovision triumph, the brothers were based in Cleveland, Ohio, USA, pursuing their careers as singers.

While Herreys continued to record and tour for a few years, they didn't replicate the massive success of their Eurovision-winning hit. Nevertheless, they played a pioneering role as the first European boyband, foreshadowing the international boyband phenomenon that would follow in the coming years. Dominating the 1980s, Herreys became Sweden's bestselling pop group, delivering over 300 live performances and gaining recognition as the first Western band to tour the Soviet Union behind the Iron

Curtain. They also shared the stage with Russian superstar Alla Pugacheva.

The three brothers reunited for a special "Diggi-Loo Diggi-Ley" performance during the intermission of one of the Swedish Melodifestivalen semifinals in 2002. Richard Herrey made a notable appearance at "Congratulations," a 50th-anniversary concert held in Copenhagen, Denmark, in October 2005. In February 2006, Richard Herrey embarked on his solo journey with the release of his first solo album, "Jag e Kung." The trio came together again for a memorable performance at the Eurovision Song Contest's Greatest Hits, a grand celebration of the show's 60th anniversary in 2015.

Diggi-Loo Diggi-Ley was overseen by Anders Engberg and Torgny Söderberg. This upbeat dance anthem, characteristic of the 1980s, featured three well-groomed young men. Notably, fellow Swedish Eurovision participant Tommy Körberg playfully labelled them "the dancing deodorants" in the press, a nickname that lingered throughout their career in Sweden. The song's nonsensical title drew parallels with previous Eurovision entries like "Boom Bang-a-Bang," "Ding-a-dong," and "La, la, la." Despite not being an immediate favourite to win, "Diggi-Loo Diggi-Ley" surprised many when it claimed victory, with bookmakers initially favouring Ireland's "Terminal 3" and Italy's "I treni di Tozeur."

According to John Kennedy O'Connor's book, "The Eurovision Song Contest – The Official History," Herrey's made history by opening the contest and becoming the third winner to sing from pole position, following Teach-In in 1975 and Brotherhood of Man in 1976.

The song's narrative centres around the lead singer stumbling upon a pair of golden shoes in the street, a discovery that propels him into a "magical world" where he feels compelled to dance. In a wishful sentiment, he desires everyone to experience the same joy. The English translation of the song, performed during their winning reprise, echoed a similar theme.

In terms of chart success, "Diggi-Loo Diggi-Ley" achieved its highest position at No.2 on the Swedish singles chart and secured the No.46 spot on the UK Singles Chart.

Leaderboard		
Year	Country	Victories
1961, 1965, 1972, 1973, 1983	Luxembourg	5
1958, 1960, 1962, 1969, 1977	France	5
1967, 1969, 1976, 1981	United Kingdom	4
1957, 1959, 1969, 1975	Netherlands	4
1974, 1984	**Sweden**	**2**
1970, 1980	Ireland	2
1978, 1979	Israel	2
1968, 1969	Spain	2
1982	Germany	1
1971	Monaco	1

Top Scores - 1984				
Country	Artist	Song	Points	Position
Sweden	Herreys	"Diggi-Loo Diggi-Ley"	145	1
Ireland	Linda Martin	"Terminal 3"	137	2
Spain	Bravo	"Lady, Lady"	106	3
Denmark	Hot Eyes	"Det' lige det"	101	4
Belgium	Jacques Zegers	"Avanti la vie"	70	5

1985

The 30th edition of the Eurovision Song Contest was held in **Gothenburg, Sweden**. The event, organised by the European Broadcasting Union (EBU) and hosted by Sveriges Television (SVT), unfolded at Scandinavium on the 4th of May 1985. The hostess for the evening was the accomplished Lill Lindfors, a former Swedish contestant.

Nineteen countries participated in the contest, and **Norway** emerged triumphant with "**La det swinge**," performed by **Bobbysocks!**, marking their inaugural victory in the competition. This achievement was particularly noteworthy considering Norway's historical struggle with low scores, including three instances of "nul points."

In addition to Greece and Israel making a return to the contest, 1985 witnessed the absence of the Netherlands due to the national Remembrance of the Dead and Yugoslavia due to the anniversary of Josip Broz Tito's death. This edition was the final one, featuring fewer than 20 participants.

Conductors played a prominent role in each performance, with 1985 being unique for featuring multiple conductors for several entries and countries. Greek conductor Haris Andreadis led the orchestra for both the Cypriot and Greek entries.

The event welcomed back 13 previous Eurovision artists, including the winner, Bobbysocks!, who had previously participated as a soloists. The presenter, Lill Lindfors, added a touch of unexpected entertainment when she experienced a wardrobe "malfunction," deliberately revealing a full-length white gown to the enthusiastic applause of the audience.

Lys Assia, the inaugural Eurovision Song Contest winner in 1956, graced the 1985 event as the guest of honour. The postcards between songs broke tradition by featuring only songwriters and composers, omitting the performing artists.

During the voting procedure, Lindfors congratulated Bobbysocks!, and Hanne Krogh and Elisabeth Andreasson responded playfully to their historic victory. The reprise of the winning entry was met with a standing ovation.

Bobbysocks is a vibrant Norwegian pop duo comprising Hanne Krogh and Swedish-Norwegian Elisabeth Andreassen - Elisabeth went by the surname Andreasson until 1994.

The duo's inception occurred in 1983, uniting two seasoned Eurovision contestants. Krogh, a three-time participant for Norway (soloist in 1971, Bobbysocks in 1985, and part of Just 4 Fun in 1991), and Andreassen, who sang for Sweden as one-half of Chips in 1982 and later triumphed with Bobbysocks, teamed up with Jan Werner Danielsen in 1994 and pursued a solo effort in 1996. Andreassen is one of only five lead artists to perform in the Eurovision Song Contest on four occasions and is among the select few to finish both first and second in Eurovision (1985 & 1996).

Bobbysocks! kickstarted their journey with the debut single "I Don't Wanna Break My Heart" (1984), released on pink-coloured vinyl. The duo's distinctive concept aimed to infuse 1950s songs with a swing mood, marrying them to a contemporary 1980s sound. This vision materialised in their first LP, "Bobbysocks!" featuring a blend of covers and new compositions.

Initially slated as the next single, "Radio" took a backseat when the duo clinched the Eurovision Song Contest with "Let It Swing," which soared to the top of the Norwegian and Belgian singles charts. In the aftermath of their Eurovision triumph, Bobbysocks! earned the prestigious Peer Gynt Prize in 1985, bestowed by Norway's parliament, the Stortinget.

The success continued with the re-release of the "Bobbysocks!" LP, now featuring "Let It Swing," attaining gold status. "Waiting for the Morning," their subsequent album released in April 1986, accompanied by the eponymous single, topped both the Norwegian singles and album charts.

Their final album, "Walkin' on Air," recorded in Los Angeles in 1987 and produced by Bill Maxwell, achieved gold status within four days, concluding a remarkable musical journey. Just before the release of "If I Fall," the lead single from the album, the duo added a touch of "decently crazy" by covering "Swing it, magister'n," a 1940 song originally sung by Swedish singer and actress Alice Babs.

After four successful years, Bobbysocks! disbanded in 1988. Nevertheless, Krogh and Andreassen continued to grace the stage together sporadically in Norway. Notably, they made an appearance at "Congratulations," the 50th-anniversary Eurovision concert in Copenhagen, Denmark, in October 2005.

In May 2010, marking the 25th anniversary of their ESC victory in 1985, Bobbysocks staged a brief comeback. They released a compilation album titled "Let It Swing - The Best Of Bobbysocks!" which included two newly recorded songs, peaking at No.13 on the Norwegian albums chart.

La det swinge ("Let it swing") pays homage to the joy of dancing to old rock 'n' roll tunes heard on the radio. Reflecting its theme, the song embraces an old-fashioned style, featuring a memorable saxophone melody at its outset. The melody arrangement exudes a retro charm, blending elements of contemporary 1980s music with nods to the 1950s. Post their win, the single ascended to the top spot on the Norwegian and Belgian singles charts and made notable appearances on charts in Denmark, Sweden, Switzerland, Austria, Ireland, and the United Kingdom.

For their Eurovision performance, Bobbysocks! members Hanne Krogh and Elisabeth Andreassen adorned sparkling, bright purple jackets over black and white outfits. Krogh donned a black-and-white striped floor-length gown. In the Eurovision Song Contest, the duo delivered the song as the thirteenth act of the night, following Italy's Al Bano and Romina Power with "Magic Oh Magic" and preceding the United Kingdom's Vikki Watson with "Love Is". When the votes were tallied, "La det swinge" secured 123 points, claiming the 1st position among 19 contestants.

Leaderboard		
Year	Country	Victories
1961, 1965, 1972, 1973, 1983	Luxembourg	5
1958, 1960, 1962, 1969, 1977	France	5
1967, 1969, 1976, 1981	United Kingdom	4
1957, 1959, 1969, 1975	Netherlands	4
1974, 1984	Sweden	2
1970, 1980	Ireland	2
1978, 1979	Israel	2
1968, 1969	Spain	2
1985	**Norway**	**1**
1982	Germany	1

Top Scores - 1985			
Country	Artist	Song	Points	Position
Norway	Bobbysocks!	"La det swinge"	123	1

EUROVISION REVISITED: CHAMPIONS VOL. I (1956-1999)

Germany	Wind	"Für alle"	105	2
Sweden	Kikki Danielsson	"Bra vibrationer"	103	3
United Kingdom	Vikki	"Love Is"	100	4
Israel	Izhar Cohen	"Olé, Olé"	93	5

1986

The Contest was hosted in **Bergen, Norway,** held at Grieghallen on the 3rd of May 1986 and presented by Åse Kleveland, a previous Norwegian Eurovision contestant.

Twenty countries participated, with Greece and Italy opting not to join, while Yugoslavia and the Netherlands made their return. Notably, Iceland made its debut in the competition this year.

Belgium emerged victorious with the song "**J'aime la vie**" by **Sandra Kim**, making her, at 13, the youngest Eurovision winner. The current age rule for participants is 16, ensuring Kim's record remains unbroken. Despite claiming to be 15 in her song's lyrics, it was later revealed that she was actually 13. Switzerland, the second-place finisher, unsuccessfully appealed for her disqualification.

The 1986 contest saw royal guests in attendance, including Crown Prince Harald, Crown Princess Sonja, Princess Märtha Louise, and Prince Haakon Magnus.

Norway, having previously been dubbed "the nul points country," took pride in hosting the event. NRK, the national broadcaster, transformed Grieghallen into a Viking-inspired "ice palace" and commissioned a special diamond-encrusted dress for the presenter Åse Kleveland.

Kleveland, a renowned folk guitarist and singer, opened the show with the multilingual "Welcome to Music." The intersong videos, known as 'postcards,' were unique, featuring actual picture postcards sent by the artists. These showcased scenic views of

Norway, along with greetings in the language of the upcoming song.

The main interval act highlighted Norwegian musicians, including Sissel Kyrkjebø and Steinar Ofsdal, accompanied by the Kringkastingsorkesteret (KORK). They showcased Bergen's traditional song, "Udsikter fra Ulriken," and presented familiar tunes while capturing the essence of the Bergen area.

Iceland's debut was made possible by RÚV's establishment of satellite television connections with the rest of Europe. However, Greece withdrew due to the contest coinciding with Holy Saturday on the Eastern Orthodox Church liturgical calendar, and Italy chose not to send a delegation to Bergen.

Sandra Kim, born on the 15th of October 1972 as Sandra Caldarone, is a Belgian singer of Italian descent. Her father, an Italian immigrant from Torrebruna in the Province of Chieti in the Abruzzo region of Italy, contributed to her diverse heritage. Kim's journey into music started in Montegnée, near Liège, where she was born to a hairdresser mother and an accordionist father. Her passion for singing emerged at the young age of seven.

Kim also represented Belgium at the Yamaha Music Festival in Tokyo in the autumn of 1986 and lent her vocals to the title song of the French animated television series Il était une fois... la vie.

Kim's musical journey continued with the release of her pop-rock album, "Make Up," on 12 May 2011. The album featured songs written by renowned Belgian artists such as Salvatore Adamo, Dani Klein (Vaya Con Dios), Ozark Henry, Anthony Sinatra (Piano Club), Jacques Duval, and David Bartholomé (Sharko). Additionally, she triumphed as "Queen" in the first season of the Belgian version of The Masked Singer.

In March 2023, Sandra Kim took on the role of a guest celebrity judge in the episode "A deux c'est mieux" of the Belgian French-language reality television series Drag Race Belgique, broadcast on Tipik.

J'aime la vie (I Love Life) - When released as a single, "J'aime la vie" dominated Belgium's singles chart for seven consecutive weeks, becoming the best-selling hit of 1986 in the country. It also made its mark internationally, reaching the top 20 in Austria, the Netherlands, Portugal, and Sweden.

The lyrics of the song, delivered in French, convey a positive message, celebrating the pleasures of life. The accompanying music video, created during Preview Week, encapsulates the theme of "things she likes." Kim joyfully engages in various activities, including participating in a physical education class, socialising with friends, enjoying music on her Walkman, indulging in a large ice cream cone, and showcasing a choreographed dance in an exercise studio. Interestingly, the video was later reconstructed scene by scene, 25 years on, for a commercial by the insurance company Delta Lloyd, presenting the old and new versions side by side.

During the Eurovision Song Contest 1986 in Bergen, the song was performed as the thirteenth act of the night, sandwiched between Ireland's Luv Bug and Germany's Ingrid Peters. With an impressive tally of 176 points, "J'aime la vie" clinched the top spot among 20 competitors.

Sandra Kim, of Italian descent, recorded her winning entry in Italian, retaining the title "J'aime la vie," and in English, with two versions titled "Crazy of Life" and "J'aime la vie."

In a 2006 online interview, Kim expressed mixed feelings about performing "J'aime la vie" at concerts, acknowledging its youthful essence and the evolution of her own preferences. Despite this, she continues to include the song in her performances, with one televised live on Norwegian TV in 2007.

Leaderboard		
Year	Country	Victories
1961, 1965, 1972, 1973, 1983	Luxembourg	5
1958, 1960, 1962, 1969, 1977	France	5
1967, 1969, 1976, 1981	United Kingdom	4
1957, 1959, 1969, 1975	Netherlands	4
1974, 1984	Sweden	2
1970, 1980	Ireland	2
1978, 1979	Israel	2
1968, 1969	Spain	2
1986	**Belgium**	1
1985	Norway	1

Top Scores - 1986			
Country	Artist	Song	Points	Position
Belgium	Sandra Kim	"J'aime la vie"	176	1
Switzerland	Daniela Simons	"Pas pour moi"	140	2
Luxembourg	Sherisse Laurence	"L'Amour de ma vie"	117	3
Ireland	Luv Bug	"You Can Count On Me"	96	4
Sweden	Lasse Holm & Monica Törnell	"E' de' det här du kallar kärlek"	78	5

1987

The 32nd Eurovision Song Contest was hosted in **Brussels, Belgium,** taking place on the 9th of May 1987, coinciding with Europe Day. The hosting duties were carried out by French-Belgian singer Viktor Lazlo and organised by the European Broadcasting Union (EBU) in collaboration with the host broadcaster Radio-télévision belge de la Communauté française (RTBF).

With **twenty-two countries** participating, including the return of Greece and Italy after their absence the previous year, this edition set a record for the highest number of competing nations up to that point. Notably, Malta, Monaco, and Morocco were the only absentees among the countries that had previously entered the competition. The significant participation posed challenges for the EBU, ranging from scheduling rehearsals to adjusting the duration of the televised finale. Subsequently, the EBU addressed this by establishing a participation limit of 22 countries after the contest. This decision sparked debates over the following five years as new and returning nations expressed interest in participating, but logistical constraints persisted.

The event unfolded at the Brussels Exhibition Centre (Brussels Expo), a collection of exhibition halls erected from 1930 on the Heysel Plateau to commemorate Belgian Independence's centenary. The Centenary Palace, serving as the main stage, stands as one of the enduring structures from the 1935 Brussels International Exposition. Presently, it continues to host trade fairs and concerts, particularly featuring prominent acts and artists.

Ireland emerged victorious with the song "**Hold Me Now**" by Johnny Logan, who secured his second Eurovision Song Contest win, having also triumphed in 1980. Logan made history as the first performer to achieve this feat.

Johnny Logan – For the artist profile, please see Logan's first Eurovision victory in 1980.

Hold Me Now unfolds as a poignant ballad, narrated from the perspective of a man grappling with the departure of his love interest. The singer implores his girlfriend to rekindle their past intimacy, urging her to "touch, touch [him] the way you used to do." Despite the melancholy farewell, the chorus encourages silence as they part ways, with the singer expressing optimism about an enduring connection despite physical separation.

Performed as the twentieth performance of the night, following Denmark's Anne-Cathrine Herdorf & Bandjo and preceding Yugoslavia's Novi Fosili, "Hold Me Now" garnered 172 points, securing the top spot in a field of 22 participants. Overwhelmed with emotion during the reprise, Logan struggled to reach the high notes, reminiscent of his 1980 victory, where he passionately declared, "I still love you, Ireland."

Recognised as one of the contest's high points, "Hold Me Now" holds the distinction of being voted the third-best song in Eurovision history by fans during the fiftieth-anniversary celebration in 2005, trailing only "Waterloo" and "Nel blu dipinto di blu."

The song's influence extended beyond its Eurovision triumph, with various artists covering it, including a reggae rendition by Tanya Stephens and a reinterpretation by Belgian rapper Kaye Styles titled "Don't Cry." McDonald's incorporated the original track into an Irish advertising campaign in 2007, featuring Logan playfully interrupting singing sessions to promote the fast-food chain's products.

In 2001, Logan released a revamped version titled "Hold Me Now 2001" as part of the album "Reach for Me," alongside a modern take on "What's Another Year 2001." This updated rendition achieved limited chart success in Denmark and Sweden.

A decade later, in his studio album "Nature of Love," Logan recorded yet another iteration of "Hold Me Now," this time titled "Hold Me Now 2010," demonstrating the enduring resonance of this iconic Eurovision winner.

Leaderboard		
Year	Country	Victories
1961, 1965, 1972, 1973, 1983	Luxembourg	5
1958, 1960, 1962, 1969, 1977	France	5
1967, 1969, 1976, 1981	United Kingdom	4
1957, 1959, 1969, 1975	Netherlands	4
1970, 1980, 1987	**Ireland**	**3**
1974, 1984	Sweden	2
1978, 1979	Israel	2
1968, 1969	Spain	2
1986	Belgium	1
1985	Norway	1

Top Scores - 1987				
Country	Artist	Song	Points	Position
Ireland	Johnny Logan	"Hold Me Now"	172	1
Germany	Wind	"Laß die Sonne in dein Herz"	141	2
Italy	Umberto Tozzi & Raf	"Gente di mare"	103	3
Yugoslavia	Novi fosili	"Ja sam za ples"	92	4
Netherlands	Marcha	"Rechtop in de wind"	83	5

1988

The contest unfolded in **Dublin, Ireland**, organised by The European Broadcasting Union (EBU) and host broadcaster Radio Telefís Éireann (RTÉ). The competition took place on the 30th of April 1988; hosting duties were shared by Irish broadcaster Pat Kenny and Miss Ireland 1980 Michelle Rocca, marking the first time since 1979 that two presenters co-hosted the event.

Twenty-one countries participated, with Cyprus initially slated to join the competition until their entry was disqualified for violating contest rules. The Cypriot song "Thimame," performed by Yiannis Dimitrou, had been presented to jurors in the country's 1984 internal selection, leading to its ineligibility. This last-minute disqualification left a field of 21, with **Switzerland** securing victory by just one point over the United Kingdom in the final vote. The winning song, "**Ne partez pas sans moi**," was performed by Canadian singer **Céline Dion**.

Dublin, Ireland's capital and largest city, provided the backdrop for the contest at the Simmonscourt Pavilion of the Royal Dublin Society, a venue typically used for agricultural and horse shows. This choice was part of Dublin's year-long celebration of its millennium, tracing its establishment back to 988 by Scandinavian settlers. The same venue had previously hosted the Eurovision Song Contest in 1981.

It's worth noting that each performance in the 1988 Eurovision Song Contest featured a conductor, except for Iceland and Italy. This added a musical dimension to the presentations, with conductors acting as maestros for the accompanying orchestra, contributing to the diverse and vibrant performances of the evening.

Céline Marie Claudette Dion CC OQ, born on the 30th of March 1968, is a Canadian singer renowned as the "Queen of Power Ballads." Recognised for her commanding and technically proficient vocals, Dion's musical repertoire spans genres such as pop, rock, R&B, gospel, and classical music. She has primarily recorded in English and French and has showcased her vocal talents in Spanish, Italian, German, Latin, Japanese, and Chinese.

Hailing from Charlemagne, Quebec, Dion was discovered by her future manager and husband René Angélil. She rose to prominence as a teenage sensation in Canada during the 1980s with a series of French-language albums. Her debut English-language album, "Unison" (1990), established her as a pop artist in North America and various English-speaking markets. "The Colour of My Love" (1993) catapulted her to global superstardom. Throughout the 1990s, Dion achieved immense success with best-selling English-language albums like "Falling into You" (1996) and "Let's Talk About Love" (1997), each certified diamond in the US with over 30 million sales worldwide.

Dion's string of international number-one hits includes memorable tracks such as "The Power of Love," "Think Twice," "Because You Loved Me," "It's All Coming Back to Me Now," "I'm Your Angel," "That's the Way It Is," "I'm Alive," and her signature song, "My Heart Will Go On," the theme for the 1997 film Titanic.

In addition to her English discography, Dion continued releasing French-language albums, with "D'eux" (1995) becoming the best-selling French-language album of all time. Her albums "S'il suffisait d'aimer" (1998), "Sans attendre" (2012), and "Encore un soir" (2016) were all certified diamond in France. In the 2000s, she solidified her reputation as a successful live performer with

"A New Day... on the Las Vegas Strip" (2003–07), the highest-grossing concert residency of all time, and the "Taking Chances World Tour" (2008–09), one of the highest-grossing concert tours of the 2000s.

Dion is celebrated as one of the greatest singers in music, with record sales exceeding 200 million worldwide. She ranks among the best-selling music artists of all time, holding the titles of the best-selling Canadian recording artist and the best-selling French-language artist in history. In 2003, the International Federation of the Phonographic Industry (IFPI) honoured her for selling over 50 million albums in Europe. Dion has won five Grammy Awards and received two Honorary Doctorates in Music degrees from Berklee College of Music and Université Laval. Billboard bestowed upon her the title of the "Queen of Adult Contemporary" for achieving the most number-one songs for a female artist. She is also the sixth all-time best-performing female soloist in Billboard 200 history.

As of the end of 2009, Dion was acknowledged by the Los Angeles Times as the top-earning artist of that decade, with combined album sales and concert revenue surpassing £747 million.

Ne partez pas sans moi (Don't Leave Without Me) was crafted by Atilla Şereftuğ and Nella Martinetti, with Dion's rendition captivated a global audience of 600 million viewers during the contest. The single, released in selected European countries in May 1988, soared to the top of the charts in Belgium, maintaining its position for an impressive three consecutive weeks.

The composition, a collaborative effort between Turkish songwriter Atilla Şereftuğ and Swiss composer Nella Martinetti, found its place on Dion's 1988 album, "The Best of Celine Dion," which saw release in chosen European territories in May 1988. In Canada, the song served as the B-side to "D'abord, c'est quoi l'amour" and was featured on the French edition of Dion's "Incognito" album. In 2005, it made a resurgence on her French compilation album, "On ne change pas." Accompanying its release was a music video in 1988, and Dion also recorded a German rendition titled "Hand in Hand."

Debuting at the summit in Belgium, the single maintained its dominance for four consecutive weeks before gradually descending to No.45. In Switzerland, it reached No.11, and in France, it secured the thirty-sixth spot. Despite selling 200,000 copies in Europe within two days and exceeding 300,000 copies overall, it stands as one of the less commercially successful Eurovision winners. Notably, it was the first winning song that was not released in the United Kingdom or Ireland. While not officially released as a single in Canada, the song entered the Quebec chart on the 1st of October 1988, enjoying a twenty-three-week presence and peaking at No.10.

Leaderboard		
Year	Country	Victories
1961, 1965, 1972, 1973, 1983	Luxembourg	5
1958, 1960, 1962, 1969, 1977	France	5
1967, 1969, 1976, 1981	United Kingdom	4
1957, 1959, 1969, 1975	Netherlands	4
1970, 1980, 1987	Ireland	3
1956, 1988	**Switzerland**	**2**
1974, 1984	Sweden	2
1978, 1979	Israel	2
1968, 1969	Spain	2
1986	Belgium	1

Top Scores - 1988				
Country	Artist	Song	Points	Position
Switzerland	Céline Dion	"Ne partez pas sans moi"	137	1
United Kingdom	Scott Fitzgerald	"Go"	136	2
Denmark	Hot Eyes	"Ka' du se hva' jeg sa'"	92	3
Luxembourg	Lara Fabian	"Croire"	90	4
Norway	Karoline Krüger	"For vår jord"	88	5

1989

The Eurovision Song Contest of 1989 marked the 34th edition of this annual musical extravaganza. It was hosted in **Lausanne, Switzerland**, following Céline Dion's triumph the previous year. The event unfolded at the Palais de Beaulieu on 6th May 1989. The charming duo of Swiss model Lolita Morena and journalist Jacques Deschenaux took centre stage as the hosts.

A total of **twenty-two countries** participated in the contest, with Cyprus making a comeback after being disqualified the previous year. **Yugoslavia** clinched victory with the song "**Rock Me**" by the Croatian band **Riva**. This triumph stands as the sole victory for Yugoslavia before its eventual breakup. Remarkably, as of 2023, they remain the last act to win the contest, performing as the final act.

The picturesque city of Lausanne, nestled in the French-speaking part of Switzerland and serving as the capital of the canton of Vaud, provided the backdrop for this musical spectacle. Situated on the shores of Lake Geneva, or Lac Léman as known in French, Lausanne faces the French town of Évian-les-Bains, with the Jura Mountains to its northwest. A mere 62 kilometres northeast of Geneva, Lausanne offered a splendid setting for the Eurovision Song Contest.

The Palais de Beaulieu, a versatile convention and exhibition centre, was selected as the host venue, which included the grand Théâtre de Beaulieu, boasting 1,844 seats and renowned as the largest theatre in Switzerland. Inaugurated in 1954, the Théâtre de Beaulieu served as a concert, dance, and theatre hall, adding a touch of grandeur to the event. The Eurovision Song Contest unfolded in the Hall 6 + 7 of the Palais, located to the right of the main hall and the theatre.

Noteworthy performances and controversies marked the event, with two participants, Nathalie Pâque and Gili Natanael, standing out for their young ages of 11 and 12, respectively. This led to the introduction of a rule by the European Broadcasting Union, stating that no performer could participate before the year of their 16th birthday—a rule that remains in force today.

The night also featured conductors leading the orchestra for each performance, except for Austria, Iceland, and Germany. In a departure from tradition, the conductors took their bows after each song, not before, creating a unique atmosphere.

The show opened with Céline Dion, the previous year's winner, treating the audience to a mimed performance of her winning song and her first English-language single, "Where Does My Heart Beat Now." This performance served as a prelude to her subsequent international success.

The notable commentary came from Ray Caruana, the lead singer of Live Report from the United Kingdom, expressing dissatisfaction at coming second to what he perceived as a less deserving song, with a narrow defeat by 7 points.

The grand finale concluded with Riva delivering their winning song, "Rock Me," in English, deviating from the Serbo-Croatian language used during the competition.

Riva - Formed in Zadar in 1986, they emerged as a Croatian pop band that made a significant impact in the music scene. The band made its debut on the stage of Zagrebfest 1988 after their formation in 1986, captivating the audience with its performance of "Zadnja Suza" ("Last Tear" in Croatian).

In the wake of their Eurovision success, Riva released two albums: "Rock Me" in 1989, named after their winning track, and "Srce Laneta" ("Deer Fawn's Heart" in Croatian) in 1990. However, the band's trajectory took an unexpected turn when they signed with a Swiss Agency for their planned third album, "Lude Glave, Lude Godine" ("Crazy Heads, Crazy Years" in Croatian). Collaborating with Per Gessle of the popular pop-rock duo Roxette, they were set to be opening acts on a world tour.

Disagreements arose when the Swiss Agency misrepresented Croatia's status as a recently independent country. The agency insisted on presenting the band as Yugoslavian for press purposes and directed their performances towards humanitarian issues in Croatia, aiding victims of the Yugoslav Wars. Feeling betrayed by the agency's portrayal amid the turmoil in their hometown, the band severed all ties.

Following this resignation, the planned album, scheduled for release, remained unreleased. Only three songs from the album surfaced during their performance at the Croatian Eurovision preselection Dora in 1993.

In 1991, Riva announced a hiatus initially intended to be short-lived, but it marked the end of the band as members focused on their personal lives. Occasional small reunions occurred between 1993 and 2016, offering glimpses of the band's legacy.

Rock Me not only clinched the Eurovision title but also propelled Yugoslav and Croatian rock into the international spotlight. Post the 1989 victory, Riva's frontwoman, Kokić, made appearances on various shows but failed to achieve significant success. During the contest, Rock Me accumulated an impressive score of 137 points. In 2022, The Independent recognised "Rock Me" as the 44th best Eurovision-winning song of all time.

EUROVISION REVISITED: CHAMPIONS VOL. I (1956-1999)

Leaderboard		
Year	Country	Victories
1961, 1965, 1972, 1973, 1983	Luxembourg	5
1958, 1960, 1962, 1969, 1977	France	5
1967, 1969, 1976, 1981	United Kingdom	4
1957, 1959, 1969, 1975	Netherlands	4
1970, 1980, 1987	Ireland	3
1956, 1988	Switzerland	2
1974, 1984	Sweden	2
1978, 1979	Israel	2
1968, 1969	Spain	2
1989	**Yugoslavia**	**1**

Top Scores - 1989				
Country	Artist	Song	Points	Position
Yugoslavia	Riva	"Rock Me"	137	1
United Kingdom	Live Report	"Why Do I Always Get It Wrong"	130	2
Denmark	Birthe Kjær	"Vi maler byen rød"	111	3
Sweden	Tommy Nilsson	"En dag"	110	4
Austria	Thomas Forstner	"Nur ein Lied"	97	5

1990

The 35th edition of this prestigious musical event was hosted in **Zagreb, SR Croatia, Yugoslavia**, organised by the European Broadcasting Union (EBU) and hosted by Jugoslavenska radiotelevizija (JRT) and Radiotelevizija Zagreb (RTZ). The competition unfolded at the Vatroslav Lisinski Concert Hall on the 5th of May 1990. Croatian television presenters Helga Vlahović and Oliver Mlakar took the stage as hosts, marking the first Eurovision Song Contest in the Balkans and the only one hosted in a communist or socialist state. **Twenty-two countries** participated, mirroring the previous year's lineup.

Italy emerged as the victor with the song "**Insieme: 1992**" by **Toto Cutugno**. At the age of 46 years and 302 days, Cutugno became the oldest winner in Eurovision history up to that point, breaking the trend of younger winners since 1958. Notably, the 1990 contest remains the last instance where the "Big Five" – Italy, France, Spain, the United Kingdom, and Germany – all secured places in the top 10 (Italy won, France tied for second, Spain came fifth, the UK came sixth, and Germany came ninth).

Zagreb, the capital of Croatia and the second-largest city in Yugoslavia, provided the backdrop for the event. The Vatroslav Lisinski Concert Hall, named after 19th-century Croatian composer Vatroslav Lisinski, hosted the contest. The venue underwent its first major renovation in 1989 to prepare for the event; subsequent reconstruction and redecoration took place in 1992, 1999, and 2009.

Despite Malta's initial plans to compete, the maximum limit of 22 participating countries prevented their entry due to no withdrawals. Musically, Spain's "Bandido" and France's "White and Black Blues" marked a new trend in Eurovision by blending contemporary dance music with ethnic influences, drawing from flamenco and calypso, respectively.

A visual shift was evident in the 1990 contest, with cameras moving dynamically from and to the stage during performances, capturing angles unseen by the live audience. Adding a touch of charm, the 1990 contest introduced Eurocat as its official mascot, a mischievous purple cat created by Joško Marušić. Eurocat appeared during the 'postcards' of each entry, offering travelogues of the respective countries, aligning with the European Year of Tourism 1990.

Notably, the 1990 Eurovision Song Contest proved to be the most profitable up until that point, marking a significant milestone in its illustrious history.

Salvatore "Toto" Cutugno entered the world on 7th July 1943, in Tendola, a borough of Fosdinovo, Lunigiana, Tuscany. Born to a Sicilian sea marshal father from Barcellona Pozzo di Gotto and a housewife mother, the family soon moved to La Spezia, Liguria, shortly after his birth.

Commencing his musical journey as a drummer, Cutugno founded his first band, Toto e i Tati, at the age of 19. He later co-founded the disco band Albatros alongside Lino Losito and Mario Limongelli. His prowess as a songwriter was evident through contributions to well-known songs for artists such as Joe Dassin, Adriano Celentano, Johnny Hallyday, Mireille Mathieu, and many others.

In 1976, Albatros participated in the Sanremo Music Festival, marking the beginning of Cutugno's successful solo career. Over the years, he participated in numerous editions of the festival, earning the moniker "the eternal second" due to several second-place finishes.

In 1980, Cutugno returned to Sanremo and emerged as the winner with the song "Solo noi" ("Only us"). However, his association with the festival is best remembered for "L'Italiano" ("The Italian"), presented in 1983. Despite finishing fifth in Sanremo, the song became Cutugno's major international hit.

In the years that followed, Cutugno continued to make significant contributions to Italian music. Notably, he received a lifetime career award at the Sanremo Festival in 2013. His influence extended beyond Italy, with performances in the United States, Australia, Germany, Spain, Romania, Turkey, and Russia.

In 2019, Cutugno faced controversy when Ukrainian politicians sought to prevent his performance in Kyiv, labelling him a "Russian war supporter in Ukraine." Despite the allegations, the concert proceeded, and Cutugno maintained his apolitical stance.

Cutugno's personal life saw him married to Carla Cutugno from 1971 until his passing. In 1990, he welcomed his only son Nico from an extramarital relationship. In 2007, Cutugno confronted a health challenge when diagnosed with prostate cancer, leading to surgery and the removal of his right kidney. He credited fellow singer Al Bano for aiding in the timely discovery of his cancer. Salvatore "Toto" Cutugno breathed his last on 22nd August 2023, succumbing to prostate cancer at the San Raffaele Hospital in Milan. His legacy endures as a symbol of Italian music on the global stage.

Insieme: 1992 ("Together: 1992") Cutugno's rendition carried a powerful message of unity, envisioning the coming together of the diverse nations of Europe. The inclusion of "1992" in the title symbolised the anticipated commencement of the European Union in that year, embodying the lyrical hope of harmonious collaboration. Adding to the richness of the performance, Cutugno was accompanied by a backing group of five singers from Slovenia, known as Pepel in kri [sl], who had previously represented Yugoslavia in 1975.

Taking the stage as the nineteenth performance of the night, "Insieme: 1992" followed Sweden's Edin-Ådahl with "Som en vind" and preceded Austria's Simone with "Keine Mauern mehr." When the votes were tallied, the song garnered an impressive 149 points, securing the first position.

Leaderboard		
Year	Country	Victories
1961, 1965, 1972, 1973, 1983	Luxembourg	5
1958, 1960, 1962, 1969, 1977	France	5
1967, 1969, 1976, 1981	United Kingdom	4
1957, 1959, 1969, 1975	Netherlands	4
1970, 1980, 1987	Ireland	3
1956, 1988	Switzerland	2
1974, 1984	Sweden	2
1978, 1979	Israel	2
1968, 1969	Spain	2
1990	**Italy**	**1**

Top Scores - 1990				
Country	Artist	Song	Points	Position
Italy	Toto Cutugno	"Insieme: 1992"	149	1
France	Joëlle Ursull	"White and Black Blues"	132	2
Ireland	Liam Reilly	"Somewhere in Europe"	132	2
Iceland	Stjórnin	"Eitt lag enn"	124	4
Spain	Azúcar Moreno	"Bandido"	96	5

1991

The contest took place on the 4th of May 1991 in **Rome, Italy,** hosted by Gigliola Cinquetti and Toto Cutugno, and the event was organised by the European Broadcasting Union (EBU) in collaboration with the host broadcaster Radiotelevisione italiana (RAI).

The chosen venue, Stage 15 of the Cinecittà Studios, was the largest film studio in Europe, known for its role in blockbuster American and Italian movies during the 1950s and 1960s.

Twenty-two countries participated in the event, with notable occurrences such as Malta's return after a sixteen-year absence and Germany's representation as a unified country post-reunification. The Netherlands opted out due to the conflict with their annual Remembrance of the Dead commemorations.

The 1991 contest witnessed a historic draw for first place, with both France and Sweden earning the same number of points. In a tie-breaker, **Sweden** emerged victorious with their entry **"Fångad av en stormvind,"** performed by **Carola**. This marked Sweden's third overall victory in the Eurovision Song Contest.

Originally intended for the Teatro Ariston in Sanremo, the contest faced challenges, including concerns about the venue's size and organisational issues. Due to geopolitical instability, particularly the Gulf War, the organisers decided to relocate the event to a more secure location, confirming Rome as the host city on the 18th of February.

Despite the late change in venue, Sanremo remained a partner, with pre-recorded footage featured during the live broadcast.

The production of the 1991 contest faced criticism for its late rehearsals, technical mishaps, and a haphazard voting sequence. However, it remains a memorable edition in the Eurovision Song Contest's rich history.

Carola Maria Häggkvist, widely known as Carola, is a prominent Swedish pop singer born on 8th September 1966 at Södersjukhuset in Stockholm. Since the early 1980s, she has been one of Sweden's most beloved performers, exploring genres from pop and disco to hymns and folk music.

Her debut album, "Främling" (1983), achieved remarkable success, selling approximately one million copies and holding the title of the biggest-selling album in Swedish music history. Carola's versatility as an artist is evident in her extensive discography, which spans various languages, including Swedish, Dutch, German, English, Norwegian, and Japanese.

Born and raised in Norsborg, south of Stockholm, Carola displayed her musical talent early on. At the age of eight, she began performing at Stockholm's Miniteatern and attended Adolf Fredrik's Music School. Carola's career witnessed various phases, from her early success in the 1980s with hits like "Mickey" and "Tommy tycker om mig" to her gospel album "My Tribute" in 1993. She explored rock-themed music with the album "Personligt" in 1994 and ventured into musical theatre, playing Maria in "The Sound of Music" in 1995.

The new millennium saw Carola's return to Eurovision in 2006 with the song "Evighet," (Eternity) later named: Invincible. Post-Eurovision, she released the album "Från nu till evighet" and continued her musical journey, exploring genres like pop, country, and gospel.

Carola's enduring career includes Christmas albums, international performances, and participation in Melodifestivalen. Despite facing challenges, such as vocal issues and controversial media attention, she remains a respected and influential figure in Swedish music.

Fångad av en stormvind (Captured by a Storm Wind) was crafted and produced by Stephan Berg. This captivating melody secured its place at No.3 on the Swedish Singles Chart and claimed the sixth spot on the Norwegian Singles Chart.

Robbert Tilli from Music & Media expressed, "Very reminiscent of one-time winner Bucks Fizz, the song is a typical example of a happy and cheerful first-prize tune."

During the Eurovision Song Contest 1991 in Rome, Carola's performance, occurring eighth in the lineup, culminated in a unique outcome. Sweden and France both garnered 146 points and received an equal number of twelve-point sets. However, Sweden clinched the victory by securing more ten-point votes—a procedure instituted to prevent a split victory, echoing the events of the Eurovision Song Contest 1969. This rule, introduced in 1991, was a one-time occurrence, making it the first and last instance of its application.

Carola's rendition of "Fångad av en stormvind" marked Sweden's third victory in the Eurovision Song Contest, following ABBA's "Waterloo" in 1974 and Herreys' "Diggi-Loo Diggi-Ley" in 1984. This victory was the second time Carola represented Sweden in Eurovision, with her earlier participation in 1983 with the song "Främling". She would later return to Eurovision in 2006 with the song "Invincible".

In addition to the original Swedish version, Carola recorded an English-language rendition of the song titled "Captured by a

Lovestorm," featuring lyrics by Richard Hampton, which made its mark on the charts in Austria, Belgium (Flanders), and The Netherlands. A remix of both versions, known as the "Hurricane Remix," was expertly crafted by Emil Hellman.

Leaderboard		
Year	**Country**	**Victories**
1961, 1965, 1972, 1973, 1983	Luxembourg	5
1958, 1960, 1962, 1969, 1977	France	5
1967, 1969, 1976, 1981	United Kingdom	4
1957, 1959, 1969, 1975	Netherlands	4
1974, 1984, 1991	**Sweden**	**3**
1970, 1980, 1987	Ireland	3
1956, 1988	Switzerland	2
1978, 1979	Israel	2
1968, 1969	Spain	2
1990	Italy	1

Top Scores - 1991				
Country	**Artist**	**Song**	**Points**	**Position**
Sweden	Carola	"Fångad av en stormvind"	146	1
France	Amina	"C'est le dernier qui a parlé qui a raison"	146	2
Israel	Duo Datz	"Kan"	139	3
Spain	Sergio Dalma	"Bailar pegados"	119	4
Switzerland	Sandra Simó	"Canzone per te"	118	5

1992

The 1992 edition took place on the 9th of May 1992 at the Malmö Isstadion in **Malmö, Sweden**. The European Broadcasting Union (EBU) and the host broadcaster, Sveriges Television (SVT), orchestrated the event, with Lydia Capolicchio and Harald Treutiger taking on the role of presenters.

A record-breaking **twenty-three countries** participated in the contest, including the return of the Netherlands after a one-year hiatus. The winner of the competition was **Ireland**, clinching victory with the song "**Why Me**," written by Johnny Logan and performed by **Linda Martin**. This marked Ireland's fourth contest win, securing Logan's third overall win as both singer and songwriter. The top five also included the United Kingdom, Malta, Italy, and Greece, with the United Kingdom securing its thirteenth second-place position. Malta and Greece secured their highest-ranking results so far.

The chosen venue contest was the Malmö Isstadion, an indoor ice hockey arena with a capacity of around 5,800 for ice hockey matches. Despite this, the contest drew an audience of approximately 3,700 spectators. This marked the third time that Sweden had hosted the Eurovision Song Contest, with previous events held in Stockholm (1975) and Gothenburg (1985).

Monaco and Morocco were the only absentees among all countries that had participated in previous editions. Noteworthy entries in the 1992 contest included the first performance in a French Creole language and the return of a song performed in Luxembourgish since 1960. The event featured several artists with previous Eurovision experience, adding a layer of familiarity and history to the competition. Sigríður Beinteinsdóttir and Grétar Örvarsson, members of Iceland's Heart 2 Heart, had previously represented the country in 1990 as Stjórnin. Rom Heck, part of Luxembourg's Kontinent in 1992, had competed in the 1989 contest as a member of the group Park Café. Linda Martin made her second contest appearance for Ireland after the 1984 contest, Mia Martini represented Italy again after 1977, and the group Wind returned for Germany, marking their third Eurovision appearance after 1985 and 1987. Additionally, Cyprus's Evridiki took the lead artist role after previously contributing backing vocals for Cypriot entries in 1983, 1986, and 1987.

Linda Martin, born in Belfast in 1952, Martin boasts a heritage blending Irish, Scottish, and Italian roots. Originally, Martini, her father's family's surname, underwent a transformation. Her paternal great-grandfather, Francis Martini, born in Dublin to Italian immigrants, had a coal-mining background from Larkhall, Scotland. Martin's maternal great-grandparents, William Green and Elizabeth Nangle, migrated to Belfast from Larkhall, Scotland, bringing a coal-mining history with them.

Martin initiated her musical journey by joining the band Chips in Omagh in 1969. They swiftly rose to prominence in Ireland's live music scene, releasing hit singles such as "Love Matters," "Twice a Week," and "Goodbye Goodbye" in the mid-to-late 1970s. In 1972, she briefly left Chips to be a vocalist with the new group Lyttle People but rejoined her former bandmates the following year. Despite numerous entries in the Irish National finals of the Eurovision Song Contest, the band continued into the 1980s. Martin departed in 1983 after winning the Castlebar Song Contest with "Edge of the Universe." She then focused on a solo career while occasionally performing live with Chips until they recruited a new lead singer, Valerie Roe, in the late 1980s.

Participating in the National Song Contest four times as a Chips member, Martin later entered the contest four times as a soloist and once as part of the group 'Linda Martin and Friends.' With nine participations, she holds the record for the most frequent entrant in the National Song Contest's history. She became one of only three artists to finish both first and second at Eurovision, alongside Lys Assia and Gigliola Cinquetti. Subsequently, only Elisabeth Andreassen and Dima Bilan have achieved this feat.

Martin presented the RTÉ quiz show The Lyrics Board, one of the broadcaster's popular formats. She also served as one of Louis Walsh's behind-the-scenes team on the first series of ITV's The X Factor. Additionally, Martin was a judge on several seasons of RTÉ's You're a Star, and on Charity You're a Star in summer 2005 and summer 2006. She participated as a guest performer at Congratulations, the 50th anniversary Eurovision concert in Copenhagen, Denmark, in October 2005. Martin was the Irish spokesperson for the Eurovision Song Contest 2007 and one of the judges for Eurosong 2009. In 2012, she mentored Jedward in the Irish Eurovision final Eurosong 2012.

During the Eurovision 2013 interval, host Petra Mede presented a lighthearted history of the contest, joking about Johnny Logan winning three times. Martin appeared in vintage footage, playfully remarking that he won the third time disguised as a woman. The joke stirred controversy, but Martin claimed to benefit from the publicity. On the same show, she performed a cover of Daft Punk's "Get Lucky."

Martin has ventured into pantomime in Dublin, starring in productions such as Cinderella, Snow White, and Robin Hood at the Olympia Theatre. She also toured Menopause the Musical with Irish entertainer Twink, although their friendship soured after an altercation in May 2010, leading to a strained relationship.

Why Me? It is a heartfelt ballad. The song gradually builds in intensity, with the singer contemplating her feelings for her lover and questioning why she is the fortunate recipient of his love over others.

During the contest, the song took the stage as the seventeenth performance, following the United Kingdom's Michael Ball with "One Step Out of Time" and preceding Denmark's Kenny Lübcke [da] & Lotte Nilsson [da] with "Alt det som ingen ser." When the votes were tallied, it amassed an impressive 155 points, securing the top spot in a field of 23 competitors.

Johnny Logan revisited the song on his 2001 album, "Reach for Me," showcasing the enduring charm of this Eurovision-winning piece.

Leaderboard		
Year	Country	Victories
1961, 1965, 1972, 1973, 1983	Luxembourg	5
1958, 1960, 1962, 1969, 1977	France	5
1970, 1980, 1987, 1992	**Ireland**	4
1967, 1969, 1976, 1981	United Kingdom	4
1957, 1959, 1969, 1975	Netherlands	4
1974, 1984, 1991	Sweden	3
1956, 1988	Switzerland	2
1978, 1979	Israel	2
1968, 1969	Spain	2
1990	Italy	1

Top Scores - 1992				
Country	Artist	Song	Points	Position
Ireland	Linda Martin	"Why Me"	155	1
United Kingdom	Michael Ball	"One Step Out of Time"	139	2
Malta	Mary Spiteri	"Little Child"	123	3
Italy	Mia Martini	"Rapsodia"	111	4
Greece	Cleopatra	"Olou tou kosmou i Elpida"	94	5

1993

The 1993 edition occurred on the 15th of May 1993; the festivities took place at the Green Glens Arena in **Millstreet, Ireland**. Orchestrated by the European Broadcasting Union (EBU) and hosted by Radio Telefís Éireann (RTÉ), the event was presented by Fionnuala Sweeney.

A record-breaking **twenty-five countries** participated, making it the largest Eurovision event at that time. Twenty-two nations from the previous year returned, with Yugoslavia notably absent due to the closure of its national broadcaster amid the Yugoslav Wars. Responding to the increased interest from former Eastern Bloc countries, a qualifying competition in Ljubljana, Slovenia, determined the participation of first-time entrants Bosnia and Herzegovina, Croatia, and Slovenia.

For the second consecutive year, **Ireland** claimed victory with the song "**In Your Eyes**," performed by **Niamh Kavanagh**. The United Kingdom, Switzerland, France, and Norway secured the remaining top five positions. Ireland's win marked their fifth overall, equalling the records held by France and Luxembourg. The venue, Millstreet's Green Glens Arena, set a unique precedent as the smallest settlement to host the event, with a population of 1,500.

Noel C Duggan, the arena's owner, generously provided the venue for free and secured an additional £200,000 from local businesses. Despite initial ridicule, Millstreet triumphed over conventional locations like Dublin and Galway due to the excellent facilities at the Green Glens Arena and the enthusiastic local community.

Given Millstreet's size, delegations were based in nearby areas such as Killarney, where receptions for participants were held at the Great Southern Hotel. The Eurovision Song Contest's expansion in the late 1980s and early 1990s, driven by the fall of communist regimes, prompted the EBU to increase the maximum number of participating countries to twenty-five.

Niamh Kavanagh was born on the 13th of February 1968 in Glasnevin, Dublin, Ireland. Kavanagh's early exposure to music came from her father, a singer and saxophonist. Influenced by artists like Aretha Franklin, Ella Fitzgerald, Blood, Sweat and Tears, and Bonnie Raitt, she often showcased her singing talent at family gatherings during her childhood.

Kavanagh's involvement in the film soundtrack for "The Commitments," where she performed as a lead and backing vocalist, preceded her Eurovision fame. However, she was unprepared for the heightened recognition that came with her later Eurovision entries.

In 1993, at the age of twenty-five, Kavanagh won the National Song Contest with "In Your Eyes," earning 118 points. This victory paved the way for her representation of Ireland at the Eurovision Song Contest in Millstreet, where she secured the top spot with 187 points.

In a remarkable return to the Eurovision stage in 2010, held in Oslo, Norway, Kavanagh represented Ireland once again with the song "It's for You." After qualifying in the semi-final, she finished 23rd in the grand final, accumulating 25 points.

Widely admired by Eurovision Song Contest enthusiasts, Kavanagh's vocal prowess has earned her acclaim. Diarmuid Furlong, president of OGAE Ireland (the official Eurovision fan club), hailed her as one of the best vocalists ever to win the contest. Despite her European success, Kavanagh remains relatively unknown in the United States, although she recorded an album there following her initial Eurovision victory.

Following her Eurovision success, Kavanagh recorded an album in Nashville, Tennessee, United States, before taking a hiatus from music to spend more time with her children.

Beyond her Eurovision engagements, Kavanagh has made various appearances, including performing at a homecoming ceremony for a Big Brother contestant, participating in national finals, and serving as the Irish spokesperson at Eurovision Song Contest 2008 and 2023.

In her personal life, Kavanagh is married to musician Paul Megahey, residing in Carrickfergus, County Antrim, Northern Ireland. The couple has two sons, Jack and Tom. Despite initially planning to move to the United States, Kavanagh changed her plans following her Eurovision success. In addition to family time, she actively engages with music sent to her and personally responds to everyone who reaches out.

In Your Eyes stands as a heartfelt love ballad composed and written by Jimmy Walsh; the song paints a narrative of the singer's journey from loneliness to finding love and heavenly solace in her lover's embrace, profoundly transforming her life.

In 1992, Walsh, based in New York, recorded a demo of the song, and the path to its Eurovision triumph took an unexpected turn when the then-unknown Idina Menzel suggested a key change for the chorus. Despite initial concerns, Menzel's conviction prevailed, resulting in a demo that caught the attention of Niamh Kavanagh. Initially hesitant about Eurovision participation, Kavanagh eventually agreed under the condition that Walsh would withdraw the song if she chose not to perform it.

Despite winning the national song contest in Ireland, Kavanagh faced challenges finding a record label due to Eurovision associations. She took matters into her own hands, partly funding the recording and releasing it in limited numbers in Ireland under the fictitious label name Eureyes Music. Simon Cowell's encounter with Kavanagh during the contest led to her signing with Arista Records, and the song received international acclaim, becoming the best-selling single in Ireland in 1993. It reached No.24 in the UK Singles Chart and achieved minor success in the Netherlands and Germany.

Leaderboard		
Year	Country	Victories
1970, 1980, 1987, 1992, 1993	**Ireland**	**5**
1961, 1965, 1972, 1973, 1983	Luxembourg	5
1958, 1960, 1962, 1969, 1977	France	5
1967, 1969, 1976, 1981	United Kingdom	4
1957, 1959, 1969, 1975	Netherlands	4
1974, 1984, 1991	Sweden	3
1956, 1988	Switzerland	2
1978, 1979	Israel	2
1968, 1969	Spain	2
1990	Italy	1

Top Scores - 1993				
Country	Artist	Song	Points	Position
Ireland	Niamh Kavanagh	"In Your Eyes"	187	1
United Kingdom	Sonia	"Better the Devil You Know"	164	2
Switzerland	Annie Cotton	"Moi, tout simplement"	148	3
France	Patrick Fiori	"Mama Corsica"	121	4
Norway	Silje Vige	"Alle mine tankar"	120	5

1994

The Contest was held on the 30th of April 1994, unfolding at the Point Theatre in **Dublin, Ireland**. The European Broadcasting Union (EBU) and host broadcaster Radio Telefís Éireann (RTÉ) organised the event, which was skillfully presented by Cynthia Ní Mhurchú and Gerry Ryan. This was the first time any nation had consecutively hosted two editions of the contest.

Twenty-five countries enthusiastically participated - As the contest continued to grow in popularity, a relegation system was introduced to prevent the lowest-scoring countries from the previous year's event from participating in the subsequent contest. This led to the exclusion of Belgium, Cyprus, Denmark, Israel, Luxembourg, Slovenia, and Turkey, making way for the debut participation of Estonia, Hungary, Lithuania, Poland, Romania, Russia, and Slovakia (Italy voluntarily abstained from participation) The contest marked a significant expansion, injecting fresh excitement into the event.

Ireland achieved an unprecedented third consecutive victory, securing a new contest record that remains unmatched as of 2023. The winning song, "**Rock 'n' Roll Kids**," crafted by Brendan Graham and performed by **Paul Harrington and Charlie McGettigan**, propelled Ireland to its sixth overall contest win. Poland, Germany, Hungary, and Malta completed the top five positions, with Poland achieving the most successful result for a debut entry in the contest's history.

A standout moment in the 1994 contest was the debut of Riverdance. Initially, a seven-minute performance featuring traditional Irish and modern music, choral singing, and Irish dancing as part of the interval act, it later evolved into a full-stage show, becoming a global phenomenon and launching the careers of lead dancers Jean Butler and Michael Flatley.

The contest was showcased at the Point Theatre in Dublin. The venue, originally a train depot and warehouse serving the nearby port, had been converted into a music venue in 1988. It underwent redevelopment and expansion in 2008 and is now known as the 3Arena. At the time of the 1994 contest, the arena could accommodate around 3,200 audience members.

Notably, four performers with previous Eurovision experience participated in the 1994 contest, adding to the diversity of the event. Marie Bergman of Sweden, Evridiki of Cyprus, Sigga of Iceland, and Elisabeth Andreasson of Norway all made triumphant returns. Additionally, backing performers from past editions, such as Rhonda Heath and Eyjólfur Kristjánsson, added their talents to the mix.

Paul Harrington, born on the 13th of May 1960, began his musical journey in Dublin, Republic of Ireland. His debut album, "What I'd Say," propelled him into the public eye, reaching the Top 10 in 1991.

During the late 1990s, Harrington became the preferred performer for numerous A-list celebrities frequenting the VIP Room at Dublin's prestigious nightspot, Lillie's Bordello. Here, he entertained and shared the stage with stars from the realms of music, film, and television. Harrington's performances extended to luminaries such as the Rolling Stones, Prince, and U2. It was at Lillie's Bordello that he reconnected with Michael Flatley after a decade, leading to a pivotal role as a principal singer in Flatley's dance extravaganza, "Celtic Tiger Live." This collaboration took Harrington to arenas across Europe and North

America, including iconic venues like Wembley and Madison Square Gardens.

In 2008, Harrington released "A Collection," and after a remarkable showcase on The Late Late Show, the album soared into Ireland's Top 20, securing the fourth position.

In 2009, he joined forces with his brothers as "The Harrington Brothers" to record "Molly Malone," the official anthem for the Leinster Rugby Team. The song topped the Irish Charts and held the number-one spot in the download charts.

The year 2010 witnessed the release of Harrington's live studio album, "Songs," featuring his unique interpretations of beloved classics. Produced by Grammy nominees Chris O'Brien and Graham Murphy, the album included collaborations with Bill Shanley, Sean Devitt, and Tony Molloy.

In 2018, Harrington unveiled a new live album titled "Lights of Home," recorded at the Sugar Club Dublin and featuring nine new songs. While this marked his first solo album in eight years, Harrington had actively collaborated on other projects during that time, including a Christmas album with the Whitefriar Street Choir ("O Holy Night") and a North American-Irish collaboration named "Cape Spear."

Beyond his musical accomplishments, Harrington has become a familiar presence on television and radio. For the past five years, he has held a regular slot on The Pat Kenny Show on Newstalk, presenting features like "The Popular Irish Ballad - a brief history" and "The Lyric's The Thing" every Tuesday morning. Harrington's radio career encompasses roles with Dublin's Q102 and Sunshine 106.8, where he contributed to presentation, scriptwriting, and voiceover work.

Throughout his illustrious career, Harrington has made numerous television appearances on shows and variety programs, including The Lyrics Board. In 2017 and 2018, he took on the role of writer and presenter for the documentary "Ireland's Eurovision Winners," released on DVD and aired on television.

In 2018, Harrington showcased his culinary skills as a guest on the popular TV show The Restaurant, earning the prestigious title of 5 Star Chef awarded by three-star Michelin chef Marco Pierre White and celebrity chef Rachel Allen.

Charles Joseph McGettigan was born on the 7th of December 1950 in Ballyshannon, County Donegal. Aside from his 1994 Eurovision performance, McGettigan also made a guest appearance as a singer at "Congratulations," Eurovision's 50th-anniversary concert.

In addition to his successful Eurovision journey, McGettigan has built an impressive discography over the years, including early works like "Songs of the Night (And Other Stories)" (1986) and "Charlie McGettigan" (1990)

The album "Rock 'N' Roll Kids - The Album" (1994) accompanied their Eurovision victory, solidifying their musical partnership. McGettigan's solo project, "In Your Old Room" (1998), offers a glimpse into his individual artistry, while "Another Side of Charlie McGettigan" (c. 2002) explores different facets of his musical style. In 2006, he released "Stolen Moments", followed by "The Man from 20" (2010) and "Some Old Someone" (Stockfisch, 2019).

In 2015, McGettigan demonstrated his songwriting prowess by penning "Anybody Got a Shoulder?" for Kat Mahon. The song was one of the five contenders in Eurosong 2015, the national selection process to determine Ireland's entry for the Eurovision Song Contest 2015. However, finished in 2nd place.

Rock 'n' Roll Kids - Penned by Brendan Graham - Despite the prevailing myth in Irish media suggesting the song was deliberately chosen not to win, with speculations about hosting responsibilities, the song defied expectations and emerged as the contest's champion.

The song, performed with McGettigan's guitar and Harrington's piano, broke new ground by being the first winning song without orchestral accompaniment. Lyrically rich, the original version featured seven verses representing various decades, but based on advice from a DJ, Graham trimmed it to maintain the song's appeal. The inspiration for the title struck Graham at a Fats Domino concert in 1991, and despite initial rejections in 1992 and 1993, it found its moment in 1994. Graham envisioned the song as an intimate kitchen conversation, drawing listeners into its narrative.

Taking the stage as the third performance of the night, "Rock 'n' Roll Kids" secured a remarkable 226 points, a groundbreaking feat in Eurovision history, surpassing the 200-point threshold.

In 2014, to celebrate the 20th anniversary of their victory, Harrington and McGettigan delivered a memorable gig at the Sugar Club in Dublin. Graham, reflecting on the song's inspiration during his Eurovision trophy acceptance, recalled the resonating piano sounds and the ambience of Bourbon Street in 1991. The legacy of "Rock 'n' Roll Kids" endures as a timeless emblem of Ireland's Eurovision success.

Leaderboard		
Year	**Country**	**Victories**
1970, 1980, 1987, 1992, 1993, 1994	Ireland	6
1961, 1965, 1972, 1973, 1983	Luxembourg	5
1958, 1960, 1962, 1969, 1977	France	5
1967, 1969, 1976, 1981	United Kingdom	4
1957, 1959, 1969, 1975	Netherlands	4
1974, 1984, 1991	Sweden	3
1956, 1988	Switzerland	2
1978, 1979	Israel	2
1968, 1969	Spain	2
1990	Italy	1

Top Scores - 1994			
Country	**Artist**	**Song**	**Points**	**Position**
Ireland	Paul Harrington & Charlie McGettigan	"Rock 'n' Roll Kids"	226	1
Poland	Edyta Górniak	"To nie ja!"	166	2
Germany	Mekado	"Wir geben 'ne Party"	128	3
Hungary	Friderika	"Kinek mondjam el vétkeimet?"	122	4
Malta	Moira Stafrace & Christopher Scicluna	"More than Love"	97	5

1995

The 1995 Eurovision Song Contest marked its 40th edition, held on the 13th of May 1995 at the Point Theatre in **Dublin, Ireland**. Organised by the European Broadcasting Union (EBU) and hosted by Radio Telefís Éireann (RTÉ), the event was presented by Mary Kennedy. This contest marked Ireland's third consecutive win.

Twenty-three countries participated; Estonia, Finland, Lithuania, the Netherlands, Romania, Slovakia, and Switzerland were replaced by Belgium, Denmark, Israel, Slovenia, and Turkey, returning after being relegated in 1993. Italy and Luxembourg declined to partake.

Norway emerged victorious with "**Nocturne**," composed by **Rolf Løvland**, written by Petter Skavlan, and performed by Secret Garden. Spain, Sweden, France, and Denmark completed the top five. Croatia and Slovenia achieved their best results, placing sixth and seventh, while Germany finished last for the fourth time.

RTÉ considered alternative venues in Galway and Limerick but chose Dublin for its cost-effectiveness. A BBC proposal to host in Belfast was rejected. RTÉ requested a rule change, accepted by the EBU, relieving them of producing the contest if Ireland won a fourth consecutive time.

Secret Garden, an Irish-Norwegian ensemble specialising in new instrumental music, is led by the duo of Irish violinist and singer Fionnuala Sherry and Norwegian composer, arranger, and pianist Rolf Løvland.

The group gained prominence by winning the 1995 Eurovision Song Contest, representing Norway with the composition "Nocturne." Over their 25-year partnership, they've achieved global success, with millions of albums sold worldwide, many attaining platinum status in various countries.

Their Eurovision success propelled their debut album, "Songs from a Secret Garden," to sell a million copies globally, achieving platinum in Norway and Korea and gold in Ireland, Hong Kong, and New Zealand. Barbra Streisand adapted "Heartstrings" from this album for her "A Love Like Ours" album and used it in her wedding to James Brolin.

Subsequent albums, "White Stones" (1997), "Dawn of a New Century" (1999), and "Once in a Red Moon" (2001), all featured success on the Billboard new-age charts. A compilation album, "Dreamcatcher," was released in 2000. In 2019, their tenth album, "Storyteller," was unveiled.

Secret Garden's renowned song "You Raise Me Up," originally performed by Johnny Logan and Brian Kennedy, has been covered by numerous artists worldwide. In 2015, Secret Garden released the autobiographical book "You Raise Me Up: The Story of Secret Garden," co-written by Rolf Løvland and Fionnuala Sherry. The book narrates their triumphs, trials, and tribulations over two decades.

Nocturne marked Norway's second triumph in the contest, the first being in 1985 with Bobbysocks!'s "Let It Swing." Secret Garden enriched their Eurovision performance with the collaboration of three guest musicians: Norwegian vocalist Gunnhild Tvinnereim, Hans Fredrik Jacobsen on the penny whistle, and Swedish nyckelharpist Åsa Jinder.

Nocturne was the fifth performance of the night, following Bosnia and Herzegovina's Davorin Popović and preceding Russia's Philip Kirkorov. It captivated the audience and the judging panel, accumulating 148 points.

Composer Rolf Løvland celebrated his second Eurovision victory, having previously written "Let It Swing." Notably, it marked the end of Ireland's four-year winning streak, setting the stage for Norway's unique tradition—humorously suggesting victories only in years ending with a 5. This light-hearted jest was acknowledged by Bobbysocks members during the Congratulations special in 2005.

Nocturne gained acclaim for its minimal lyrics, with only 24 words in the original Norwegian version. The majority of the composition featured a mesmerising violin intermezzo performed by Irish musician Fionnuala Sherry. This unique approach set it apart, with Finland later echoing a similar style in 1998 with "Aava."

Released exclusively in Europe and Scandinavia, "Nocturne " reached impressive chart positions. It topped the charts in Israel for four weeks and secured positions such as No.6 in Flanders, No.7 in Ireland, and No.20 in the Netherlands. In the UK, it reached No.90 on the Singles Chart in October 1995.

Critics praised " Nocturne" for its musical depth, with Music & Media highlighting its victory as a triumph of music over fast food. Alan Jones from Music Week appreciated its haunting and pastoral qualities, attributing its uniqueness to Fionnuala Sherry's Gaelic influence.

Adding a touch of comedy, the song was covered by the country-inspired novelty band Dusty Cowshit. Their version reached No.16 on the Norwegian Singles Chart in 1996.

Leaderboard		
Year	Country	Victories
1970, 1980, 1987, 1992, 1993, 1994	Ireland	6
1961, 1965, 1972, 1973, 1983	Luxembourg	5
1958, 1960, 1962, 1969, 1977	France	5
1967, 1969, 1976, 1981	United Kingdom	4
1957, 1959, 1969, 1975	Netherlands	4
1974, 1984, 1991	Sweden	3
1956, 1988	Switzerland	2
1978, 1979	Israel	2
1968, 1969	Spain	2
1985, 1995	**Norway**	**2**

Top Scores - 1995				
Country	Artist	Song	Points	Position
Norway	Secret Garden	"Nocturne"	148	1
Spain	Anabel Conde	"Vuelve conmigo"	119	2
Sweden	Jan Johansen	"Se på mej"	100	3
France	Nathalie Santamaria	"Il me donne rendez-vous"	94	4
Denmark	Aud Wilken	"Fra Mols til Skagen"	92	5

1996

The 1996 Eurovision Song Contest undertook its 41st edition on the 18th of May at the Oslo Spektrum in **Oslo, Norway**. Organised by the European Broadcasting Union (EBU) and hosted by Norsk rikskringkasting (NRK), the event was presented by Ingvild Bryn and Morten Harket.

Thirty countries submitted entries, and a non-public, audio-only qualifying round took place two months before the final to trim the number down to **twenty-three countries**. Denmark, Germany, Hungary, Israel, Macedonia, Romania, and Russia were subsequently eliminated, leading to Germany's absence from the contest for the first time.

Ireland emerged victorious with the song "**The Voice**," written by Brendan Graham and performed by **Eimear Quinn**. This marked Ireland's seventh contest win, extending their record and securing their fourth win in five years. The top five also included Norway, Sweden, Croatia, and Estonia, with Croatia, Estonia, and Portugal achieving their best results to date by placing sixth. The 1996 contest was the last to determine results solely through jury voting, paving the way for widespread adoption of televoting from 1998 onwards.

Initially, broadcasters from thirty-three countries expressed interest, but entries from Bulgaria, Moldova, and Ukraine did not materialise.

Noteworthy performers included Marianna Efstratiou, representing Greece for the second time; Elisabeth Andreassen, making her fourth appearance after previous stints with Sweden and Norway; and Georgina Abela, returning as a backing singer for Malta after representing the country in 1991.

Leaderboard		
Year	Country	Victories
1970, 1980, 1987, 1992, 1993, 1994, 1996	**Ireland**	**7**
1961, 1965, 1972, 1973, 1983	Luxembourg	5
1958, 1960, 1962, 1969, 1977	France	5
1967, 1969, 1976, 1981	United Kingdom	4
1957, 1959, 1969, 1975	Netherlands	4
1974, 1984, 1991	Sweden	3
1956, 1988	Switzerland	2
1978, 1979	Israel	2
1968, 1969	Spain	2
1985, 1995	Norway	2

Top Scores - 1996				
Country	Artist	Song	Points	Position
Ireland	Eimear Quinn	"The Voice"	162	1
Norway	Elisabeth Andreassen	"I evighet"	114	2
Sweden	One More Time	"Den vilda"	100	3
Croatia	Maja Blagdan	"Sveta ljubav"	98	4
Estonia	Maarja-Liis Ilus and Ivo Linna	"Kaelakee hääl"	94	5

1997

This Eurovision Song Contest marked the 42nd edition of this annual event, held on the 3rd of May 1997 at the Point Theatre in Dublin, Ireland. The European Broadcasting Union (EBU) and host broadcaster Radio Telefís Éireann (RTÉ) crafted the event, with Carrie Crowley and Ronan Keating as presenters. Notably, it was the seventh and last edition staged in Ireland and the fourth produced by RTÉ in five years. The Point Theatre, the host venue for the third time, set a record as the only venue to host three Eurovision Song Contests, having previously hosted in 1994 and 1995.

Twenty-five countries participated, and a new relegation system determined eligibility based on each country's average points from previous contests. Italy returned after a hiatus in 1993, and Denmark, Germany, Hungary, and Russia rejoined after skipping the 1995 contest. Belgium, Finland, and Slovakia were excluded due to new relegation rules.

The **United Kingdom** emerged victorious with "**Love Shine a Light**" by **Katrina and the Waves**, written by Kimberley Rew. Ireland, Turkey, Italy, and Cyprus rounded out the top five. Televoting, introduced by five countries, allowed public participation in results for the first time. Additionally, entries were permitted to feature no live music accompaniment, using only backing tracks.

The 1997 contest left a lasting impact on Eurovision, featuring the first openly LGBT artist, Paul Oscar from Iceland, and influencing future editions with changes like abandoning live musical accompaniment. A successful televoting trial in five countries led to its widespread adoption in 1998.

Noteworthy participants included Şebnem Paker for Turkey and Maarja-Liis Ilus, competing solo for Estonia after a previous duet in Oslo. Alma Čardžić made her second appearance, having represented Bosnia and Herzegovina in 1994.

Katrina and the Waves, a renowned UK rock band, gained fame with their 1985 hit "Walking on Sunshine." The band's roots trace back to 1975 when guitarist Kimberley Rew and drummer Alex Cooper founded The Waves in Cambridge, England. In 1978, Katrina Leskanich joined the pop cover band Mama's Cookin' as a vocalist and keyboard player, alongside Vince de la Cruz on vocals and lead guitar. By 1980, Cooper had joined Mama's Cookin' on drums, and the band started performing in England. The reunion of Rew and Cooper in 1981 led to the transformation of Mama's Cookin' into The Waves, with Leskanich assuming the role of lead vocalist.

In 1982, the band released their debut EP, "Shock Horror!" and rebranded as Katrina and the Waves. The turning point came in 1983 with the release of their album "Walking on Sunshine" in Canada, garnering both critical acclaim and commercial success. By 1985, they signed with Capitol Records and released their international debut album, featuring the iconic single "Walking on Sunshine." Although their subsequent album, "Waves," didn't replicate the same success, the band continued touring and releasing new music.

In 1998, Leskanich's departure due to internal conflicts triggered legal battles that prohibited her from using the band's name. Despite attempts to find a replacement, the remaining members decided to disband in 1999, redirecting their focus to individual careers.

In 2005, Leskanich co-hosted the Congratulations: 50 Years of the Eurovision Song Contest alongside Renārs Kaupers. She opened the show by singing her winning song, surrounded by flag holders representing all nations that had ever participated in Eurovision. The commemorative anniversary event took place at the Forum in Copenhagen on 22 October 2005, with Danmarks Radio (DR) as the host broadcaster. During the UK selection process's final in 2008, Eurovision: Your Decision featured a remix of her song. In 2009, Leskanich performed it alongside the Dutch SuperVoices, composed of 2000 Dutch choir singers. She also showcased the song in the UK's Eurovision selection process, Eurovision: You Decide, in 2016 on BBC Four.

On the 15th of December 2019, Leskanich presented the song at Het Grote Songfestivalfeest, a Dutch live television concert programme featuring Eurovision Song Contest artists. It served as a prelude to the Eurovision Song Contest 2020, initially scheduled for Rotterdam, the Netherlands, in May 2020. Following the cancellation of the 2020 contest due to the COVID-19 pandemic, the organisers arranged the replacement show, Eurovision: Europe Shine a Light. The title of the show was inspired by Leskanich's song. During the event, the Rotterdam Philharmonic Orchestra delivered an orchestral rendition of the song, and towards the end of the show, Leskanich performed it once again alongside all the artists slated for the cancelled contest (except Hooverphonic from Belgium), concluding the memorable event.

Love Shine a Light garnered an average of 9.458 points per country, constituting 78.82% of the total votes available. This achievement ranks as the third-highest in the history of the current voting system, trailing only "Save Your Kisses for Me" by Brotherhood of Man in 1976 (9.647 points per jury, 80.39% of available points) and "Ein bißchen Frieden" by Nicole in 1982 (9.470 votes per jury, 78.91% of available points).

Additionally, the song received maximum points from ten out of twenty-four countries, marking a notable 41.7%. This places it as the fourth-highest in this category, surpassed by "Euphoria" by Loreen in 2012 (which received 12 points from eighteen out of forty-one countries, or 43.9%), "Non ho l'età" by Gigliola Cinquetti in 1964 (earning the then-maximum 5 points from eight out of fifteen countries, or 53.3%), and "Ein bißchen Frieden" in 1982 (12 points from nine out of seventeen countries, or 52.9%).

Leaderboard		
Year	Country	Victories
1970, 1980, 1987, 1992, 1993, 1994, 1996	Ireland	7
1967, 1969, 1976, 1981, 1997	**United Kingdom**	**5**
1961, 1965, 1972, 1973, 1983	Luxembourg	5
1958, 1960, 1962, 1969, 1977	France	5
1957, 1959, 1969, 1975	Netherlands	4
1974, 1984, 1991	Sweden	3
1956, 1988	Switzerland	2
1978, 1979	Israel	2
1968, 1969	Spain	2
1985, 1995	Norway	2

Top Scores - 1997				
Country	Artist	Song	Points	Position
United Kingdom	Katrina & the Waves	"Love Shine a Light"	227	1
Ireland	Marc Roberts	"Mysterious Woman"	157	2
Turkey	Şebnem Paker & Grup Ethnic	"Dinle"	121	3
Italy	Jalisse	"Fiumi di parole"	114	4
Cyprus	Hara & Andreas Konstantinou	"Mana mou"	98	5

1998

The 1998 Eurovision Song Contest marked the 43rd edition of this annual event, which took place on 9th May 1998 at the National Indoor Arena in **Birmingham, United Kingdom**. The European Broadcasting Union (EBU) organised the contest, with the British Broadcasting Corporation (BBC) serving as the host broadcaster. The event was presented by Terry Wogan and Ulrika Jonsson.

Twenty-five countries participated, with six nations absent from the 1997 edition due to low average points totals over the previous five contests. Austria, Bosnia and Herzegovina, Denmark, Iceland, and Russia were relegated, while Italy chose not to participate. Macedonia made its first contest appearance, filling one of the vacant spots along with previously relegated and absent countries Belgium, Finland, Israel, Romania, and Slovakia.

The winning song was "**Diva**" from **Israel,** performed by **Dana International**. The top five also included the United Kingdom, Malta, the Netherlands, and Croatia. Dana International, the winner, was the first openly transgender participant in the contest and the first openly LGBTQ+ winning artist. However, her participation sparked controversy in Israeli society, leading to opposition and death threats before the event.

Notably, the 1998 contest was the first to use televoting to determine results predominantly. It also marked the last time participants were required to perform in the language of their country and the final contest featured an orchestra and live music accompaniment for competing entries.

Birmingham was selected as the host city, and the National Indoor Arena served as the venue. The UK had previously hosted the Eurovision Song Contest seven times, with Birmingham setting a new record as the eighth host city. The selection of the host city followed visits to various cities across the UK, with Belfast, Birmingham, Cardiff, Glasgow, London, and Manchester shortlisted. Birmingham's National Indoor Arena was officially announced as the host venue on 8th August 1997.

The contest also saw changes in participant eligibility, with a relegation system introduced in 1993 to manage the high number of countries wishing to enter. The relegation rules, based on each country's average points total in previous contests, were used again ahead of the 1998 event. Austria, Bosnia and Herzegovina, Denmark, Germany, Iceland, and Russia were initially excluded, but after Italy declined to participate, Germany was allowed to enter. The relegation calculations considered the average points total and total points scored in the most recent contest to determine the final order.

Sharon Cohen (professionally known as **Dana International**) was born on 2nd February 1969 in Tel Aviv, Israel; her musical journey includes eight albums and three compilation albums.

Dana's early life in Tel Aviv was marked by her identification as a female from a young age. Despite financial challenges, her mother supported her passion for singing, and she came out as transgender at the age of 13. Her stage name, Dana International, is a feminised version of her childhood friend Daniel, who tragically passed away in a car accident.

In the early 1990s, Dana gained recognition as a drag queen, parodying famous female singers. Offer Nissim, a well-known Israeli DJ, discovered her during a performance, leading to the production of her debut single, "Saida Sultana." In 1993, Dana underwent male-to-female sex reassignment surgery in London and legally changed her name to Sharon Cohen.

Her debut album, "Danna International," released in 1993, became a gold record in Israel and garnered international attention. Subsequent albums like "Umpatampa" (1994) and "Maganuna" (1996) contributed to her rising popularity. In 1998, Dana faced opposition from conservative groups when chosen to represent Israel in Eurovision.

In the late '90s and early 2000s, Dana released albums like "Free" (1999) and "Yoter Ve Yoter" (2001). Despite a hiatus from show business, she made a comeback with the album "Hakol Ze Letova" (2007) and participated in Eurovision 2008 as a songwriter.

Dana's later career involved diverse projects, including judging the Israeli music talent contest "Kokhav Nolad," releasing singles like "HaKol Ze LeTova" (2007), and representing Israel at Eurovision 2011 with "Ding Dong."

In 2013, Dana released new singles like "Ma La'asot" and later appeared as a judge on the music reality show "Yeshnan Banot." Her continuous engagement in the music scene includes performances, releases, and collaborations, maintaining her presence on both national and international platforms.

Dana International remains a trailblazer, using her platform to advocate for tolerance and acceptance, especially in matters of gender identity and equality. Her impactful contributions to the music industry and unwavering resilience make her a notable figure in Israel's cultural landscape.

Diva holds the distinction of being the last winning entry in a language other than English until 2007. Notably, it marked the finale of live orchestral accompaniment in the contest, with the subsequent 1999 edition lacking the budget and venue capacity for such a musical ensemble.

The melody was crafted by Svika Pick and intertwined seamlessly with the poignant lyrics penned by Yoav Ginai. Offer Nissim took charge of the song's production, with Alon Levin contributing to the music arrangements. The track found its place on Dana International's fifth album, "Free" (1999). This victory marked Israel's third in the Eurovision Song Contest, a significant achievement following their consecutive triumphs in 1978 and 1979. Dana International's win is etched in Eurovision history as a groundbreaking moment.

The performance itself featured Dana International adorned in a silver dress, supported by four other female singers clad in black, with no elaborate choreography.

Positioned as the eighth entry of the night, following Poland and preceding Germany, "Diva" amassed 172 points at the close of voting, securing the coveted 1st place in a field of 25 participants. Remarkably, Israel's triumph followed a year of absence in the competition, an unusual feat that added to the historical significance of the win.

Dana International's flamboyant late arrival for the results presentation, coupled with an extravagant costume designed by Jean-Paul Gaultier adorned with bird feathers, added an extra layer of spectacle to the occasion.

In a 2005 internet poll conducted by the European Broadcasting Union, "Diva" earned a spot as one of the 14 most popular songs in Eurovision history. It took the stage once again at the Congratulations 50th anniversary concert in Copenhagen, Denmark, in October 2005.

Despite its status as a cherished Eurovision winner, "Diva" remained unavailable on digital music platforms until 2019, except for Scandinavia. Efforts to secure digital release rights proved successful, with the English version released on 11th April 2019 and the Hebrew version following a week later.

"Diva" presents a moderately uptempo composition, paying homage to powerful women of history and mythology. The lyrics name-drop iconic figures such as Victoria, the Roman goddess of victory or Queen Victoria, Aphrodite, the Greek goddess of beauty and love; and the legendary Greek queen Cleopatra. The song's content exudes a celebratory ode to the strength and influence of remarkable women across the ages.

Leaderboard		
Year	Country	Victories
1970, 1980, 1987, 1992, 1993, 1994, 1996	Ireland	7
1967, 1969, 1976, 1981, 1997	United Kingdom	5
1961, 1965, 1972, 1973, 1983	Luxembourg	5
1958, 1960, 1962, 1969, 1977	France	5
1957, 1959, 1969, 1975	Netherlands	4
1978, 1979, 1998	**Israel**	**3**
1974, 1984, 1991	Sweden	3
1956, 1988	Switzerland	2
1968, 1969	Spain	2
1985, 1995	Norway	2

Top Scores - 1998				
Country	Artist	Song	Points	Position
Israel	Dana International	"Diva"	172	1
United Kingdom	Imaani	"Where Are You?"	166	2
Malta	Chiara	"The One That I Love"	165	3
Netherlands	Edsilia	"Hemel en aarde"	150	4
Croatia	Danijela	"Neka mi ne svane"	131	5

1999

The 44th edition was hosted on the 29th of May 1999 at the International Convention Centre in **Jerusalem, Israel**, organised by The European Broadcasting Union (EBU) and the Israel Broadcasting Authority (IBA). This contest introduced a trio of presenters, including singer Dafna Dekel, radio and television presenter Yigal Ravid, and model and television presenter Sigal Shachmon, making it the first edition with three hosts in a single show. Dekel, who had previously represented Israel in the 1992 contest, achieved a sixth-place finish with the song "Ze Rak Sport".

A total of **twenty-three countries** participated, with Finland, Greece, Hungary, Macedonia, Romania, Slovakia, and Switzerland not taking part due to relegation or their choice not to return. Austria, Bosnia and Herzegovina, Denmark, and Iceland returned to the contest after their last participation in 1997, while Lithuania made its first appearance since 1994.

Sweden emerged as the winner with the song "**Take Me to Your Heaven**," performed by **Charlotte Nilsson**. Iceland, Germany, Croatia, and Israel secured the top five positions. Notably, this edition allowed countries to perform in the language of their choice, a departure from the previous requirement. Additionally, it was the first contest without an orchestra or live music accompanying the entries.

The event took place at the International Convention Centre in Jerusalem, Israel, the same venue as the 1979 contest. The choice of location faced protests from the Orthodox Jewish community, but financial guarantees from the Israeli government ensured the contest stayed in Israel, despite considerations of moving it to Malta or the United Kingdom.

In the aftermath of the contest, a compilation album featuring many of the participating entries was released in Israel. Commissioned by IBA and distributed through the Israeli record label IMP Records, the album included nineteen of the twenty-three competing acts on CD. Additionally, a video CD accompanied the release, featuring clips from the televised broadcast and backstage footage.

Anna Jenny Charlotte Perrelli, born on the 7th of October 1974 and initially known as Charlotte Nilsson until 2003, is a prominent Swedish singer and television host.

Born in Hovmantorp, in southern Sweden's Småland province, Perrelli began her musical journey at thirteen by joining a local dansband, Bengt Ingvars, which later became "Bengt Ingvars med Charlotte." After completing her compulsory school education, she moved to Växjö, attending the High School of Performing Arts. During this time, she also served as the lead singer for the band Kendix.

In 1994, Perrelli joined the established dansband Anders Engbergs, later moving to the highly successful Wizex in 1997. The band's increased reputation led to a Grammy nomination in 1998 for the album "Mot nya mål," and the gold-certified album "Tusen och en natt."

Apart from her music career, Perrelli starred as Millan Svensson in the Swedish soap opera "Vita lögner" from 1997 to 1998.

After winning Melodifestivalen in 1999, Perrelli represented Sweden in the Eurovision Song Contest with "Take Me to Your Heaven," securing victory with 163 points. Following this success, she toured Europe and the Middle East, promoting her winning song. She also began work on her debut solo album, titled "Charlotte."

In 2001, Perrelli released her second album, "Miss Jealousy," which included the hit single "You Got Me Going Crazy." She promoted the album throughout Europe and New Zealand. Renaming herself Charlotte Perrelli after her 2003 marriage, she released the single "Broken Heart" in September 2003, followed by the album "Gone Too Long" in June 2004.

After hosting Melodifestivalen 2004, Perrelli continued her success with the release of her most successful album, "Gone Too Long," in mid-2004. She toured with Robert Wells and participated in TV shows like "Inför Eurovision." In 2006, she released the album "I din röst," paying tribute to jazz singer Monica Zetterlund.

In 2008, Perrelli won Melodifestivalen again with the song "Hero." Despite being a favourite, she finished 18th in the Eurovision Song Contest. Her album "Hero" went platinum in Sweden. She toured with Wells and signed a record deal in China. She released her Christmas album "Rimfrostjul" in 2008 and continued her involvement in TV shows and judging roles.

Perrelli announced a new album in 2010 but released it in 2012. She recorded a single for the Swedish Royal Wedding in 2010 and released a fitness book in August. Her Christmas album "Min barndoms jul" came out in 2013. In 2015, she released "Bröllopsvalsen" and a book about pregnancy. In 2017, she released the album "Mitt liv" and continued touring with Diggiloo. She participated in Melodifestivalen 2021 with the song "Still Young" and reached the final.

Take Me to Your Heaven was globally released on the 21st of June 1999, produced by Mikael Wendt, and achieved notable positions on various singles charts. It reached No.2 in Sweden, No.5 in Flemish Belgium, No.10 in Norway, No.20 in the United Kingdom, and No.23 in the Netherlands.

On the 24th of April 1999, the Swedish version of the song entered the radio chart Svensktoppen, claiming the number-one spot and maintaining its dominance for eight consecutive weeks until the 4th of September 1999.

The content of the song revolves around the theme of love, delivering an upbeat message as the singer implores her lover to transport her to heaven through their love. Some fans have drawn parallels between this entry and the 1974 Swedish winner by ABBA. The music video complements the song's atmosphere, set against a wintry backdrop with Charlotte Nilsson gracefully walking in the snow.

Leaderboard		
Year	Country	Victories
1970, 1980, 1987, 1992, 1993, 1994, 1996	Ireland	7
1967, 1969, 1976, 1981, 1997	United Kingdom	5
1961, 1965, 1972, 1973, 1983	Luxembourg	5
1958, 1960, 1962, 1969, 1977	France	5
1974, 1984, 1991, 1999	**Sweden**	**4**
1957, 1959, 1969, 1975	Netherlands	4
1978, 1979, 1998	Israel	3
1956, 1988	Switzerland	2
1968, 1969	Spain	2
1985, 1995	Norway	2

Top Scores - 1999				
Country	Artist	Song	Points	Position
Sweden	Charlotte Nilsson	"Take Me to Your Heaven"	163	1
Iceland	Selma	"All Out of Luck"	146	2
Germany	Sürpriz	"Journey to Jerusalem – Kudüs'e Seyahat"	140	3
Croatia	Doris	"Marija Magdalena"	118	4
Israel	Eden	"Happy Birthday"	93	5

Disclaimer

The author is not responsible for any errors or omissions or for any actions taken based on the information contained in this book. This book is provided for informational purposes only, and the author and publisher shall not be liable for any errors or omissions, or for any actions taken based on the information contained in this book.

**Coming Soon: Eurovision Revisited:
Champions Vol 2 (2000 and beyond)**

**Also Available: Eurovision Revisited:
A Guide to the United Kingdom**